From Page to Stage

From Page to Stage

HOW THEATRE DESIGNERS MAKE CONNECTIONS BETWEEN SCRIPTS AND IMAGES

Rosemary Ingham

Heinemann
Portsmouth, NH

Heinemann
A division of Reed Elsevier Inc.
361 Hanover Street
Portsmouth, NH 03801-3912

Offices and agents throughout the world

Library of Congress Cataloging-in-Publication Data
Ingham, Rosemary.
From page to stage : how theatre designers make connections between scripts and images / by Rosemary Ingham.
p. cm.
ISBN 0-435-07042-8
1. Theaters—Stage setting and scenery. 2. Drama—Explication. I. Title.
PN2091.S8I45 1997
792'.025—dc21 97-22412
CIP

Editor: Lisa A. Barnett
Production: J. B. Tranchemontagne, Abigail M. Heim
Design: Mary C. Cronin
Cover design: Michael Leary
Manufacturing: Louise Richardson

Printed in the United States of America on acid-free paper
02 01 00 ML 2 3 4 5

For

Keith Belli

1956–1996

Contents

Preface

This book is about the nature of the relationship between playscripts and theatre designers. I believe that the playwright's words lie at the absolute center of every fully realized production of a play. Those words constitute the implicit or explicit subject of every conversation that takes place between directors, designers, performers, and other members of all producing groups. The playwright's words are also the subject of the dialogue that takes place between the production and the audience every time a play is performed, the dialogue that is the heart of every theatrical event.

Good conversations happen when people listen to each other, think before they respond, respect each other's opinions, and know what they're talking about. The aim of this book is to explore the ways in which theatre designers prepare themselves to take strong, active roles in production collaborations by first entering into fruitful conversations with the playscripts themselves.

Theatre designers create with images; playwrights create with words. During the process of reading and hearing the words on the pages of a playscript, a theatre designer quite naturally begins to have a series of exploratory thought conversations with the characters in the play (who are usually humans but may also be gods, animals, ideas, or even teacups), and with the playwright (who may be alive and well and working on rewrites, or may have died in ancient times). As these thought conversations develop, the designer thinks (discovers, imagines) images. It is a magical process. But because theatre designers engage in this magical process on a daily basis, most of us take it for granted. We only puzzle over its mysterious and complex qualities when we get stuck or when we attempt to explain the process aloud. In those instances, we discover to our dismay that the script-to-design process does not lend itself easily to words.

There are definite pitfalls inherent in using words to describe a visually dominant process. I have tried to step carefully around the most obvious of these pitfalls. I have, whenever possible, included drawings and pictures to illustrate the ways the words of scripts inspire theatre designers to think up rooms, furniture, shaped spaces, dresses, lamps, hats, qualities of light, buckets, baskets, and trousers—all the specifics that in successful productions become inseparable from the words on the page, and that together with them produce a living, breathing, glowing, vibrant, three-dimensional play. Even the most evocative production photograph, however, is not much help when we try to understand how a playscript influences the way the actual process of design. Nor does it help us to see, when we examine the relationships between the design and the script after the fact, why that particular process worked. Therefore, I depend largely on words to evoke the magical process that creates the connections between dramatic writing and the designer's imagination, and that results in consistently coherent, and sometimes downright brilliant, theatrical designs.

Rosemary Ingham

Acknowledgments

I am grateful to all of my family, friends, colleagues, and students, who have listened patiently while I talked myself into believing I might find words to express the connections between plays on the page and designs on the stage. Special thanks are due to Helen Housley, Gregg Stull, Kurt Daw, and my editor, Lisa Barnett.

Four theatre designers have been especially helpful to me as I worked my way through this book. They have answered questions, discussed with me their individual approaches to design, allowed me, by way of audio and videotapes, to listen in on their design conferences, and contributed significantly to the visual portion of the book. I simply could not have done this work without them. Thank you Keith Belli, Jamie Bullins, Liz Stillwell, and Paul Tazewell.

From Page to Stage

Imagination, Perception, and Memory

1

> [T]here are three discernible types of imaging: There is thinking with images, or illustrated supposing; there is thinking through images, or interior dramatic rehearsal; and there is thinking in images, or being an internal spectator.
>
> Eva T. H. Brann, *The World of the Imagination*

Once, when my eighteen-month-old grandson, Nathan, was visiting my house, I interrupted his progress toward the top of a short flight of stairs leading down to the front door and warned him that he was in danger of falling. I said: "If you get too close to that top step, you might fall down the stairs and hit your head on the floor." Nathan, who had stopped when I spoke to him, looked down the stairs. As I watched, I saw his face reflect what he was seeing in his mind: his body falling through space. At, I suspect, the moment of imaged impact, Nathan closed his eyes, opened his mouth, and began to scream. After his mother and I had comforted him, I reflected on the powerful, dramatic result—fear bordering on terror—of the image, or images, appearing somewhere behind Nathan's eyes in what we usually call the mind. The image was not based on actual experience because Nathan had never fallen down the stairs in my house or any other set of stairs. My words describing what might happen if he fell had created the image in his mind. As I continued to think about the incident, I also realized that my impulse to warn Nathan was not based on actual experience. No child had ever fallen down the stairs in my house; indeed, I had never actually seen any child fall down any stairs. I was simply responding to a possibility I knew existed: an eighteen-month-old child could fall down the stairs and be seriously hurt. The entire incident occurred because all humans, young and old, have an innate ability we call the power of the imagination to see things they have not actually seen, think thoughts they have not previously heard or read, and even understand concepts they have not been specifically taught.

Nathan's experience, although terrifying for him, was an ordinary, garden-variety encounter with imagination. It is the kind of projected imaging that occurs somewhere in our heads (which is where we intuitively place such events) all the time. We do not, for example, have to have been involved in a head-on car collision to imagine ourselves in one. We know the potential for head-on collisions exists even if we have never seen photographs, films, or videotapes of such collisions. Not only do we understand that collisions are possible, we can readily imagine what a collision might do to our automobiles and to ourselves. On the other hand, we are also equally well equipped to imagine ourselves traveling safely down any and all roads, avoiding every potential collision.

Even though imagination is part of our basic human apparatus, the ways in which imagination works remain mysterious. What incites the imagination? Where do the mental pictures—the images—come from? What is the relationship between knowing and imagining? Do we know the potential results of collisions because we can imagine them? Or do we imagine the results of collisions because we know what can happen to cars and human bodies? Is it more important for the safe driver to imagine collisions or the absence of collisions?

Most important of all, since the subject of this book is designing for the theatre, what in the world is the relationship between the mental phenomenon called imagination, which appears to help protect us from falling downstairs and engaging in head-on car crashes, and the mental phenomenon called imagination, said to be the engine that sparks, fuels, and motivates creativity?

- Overheard at the Museum of Modern Art, from a young man staring at Picasso's *Three Musicians*: "Man, that dude had one overactive imagination!"
- Said to the parent of a child who regularly draws pictures of blue cows with wings, six-legged purple dogs, and humans with two heads: "Lee is the most imaginative child in the class."
- Thought by the theatre design student struggling to come up with at least one idea for the next day's project, a preliminary color scheme for Ibsen's *Ghosts*: "Where is my imagination when I need it?"

In the introduction to her exhaustive and challenging book, *The World of the Imagination*, Eva T. H. Brann offers three brief definitions of the imagination from three different perspectives:

> In philosophy, the core definition of the imagination is that it is a powerful mediating between the senses and the reason by virtue of representing perceptual objects without their presence.
>
> In psychology, the preference is for defining the class of representations, that is, the mental imagery, rather than the faculty. Mental imagery is a quasi-sensory or quasi-perceptual experience which occurs in the absence of the usual external stimuli and which may be expected to have behavioral consequences different from those attendant on their sensory counterpart.
>
> In ordinary discourse, finally, the imagination is most likely to be defined straightforwardly as a capacity for seeing things in one's head—the aforementioned "mind's eye."

In other words, some people are particularly interested in the mental faculty that allows us to produce images, others are fascinated by the nature of the images themselves, while most of us simply go about our daily tasks seeing, learning from, being frightened by, enjoying, dreading, drawing pictures, and making three-dimensional representations of the things that mysteriously appear somewhere behind or beyond our eyes.

Reading and exploring a dramatic text and using (or allowing) the results of that exploration to inform the process and the products of theatre design are activities carried out largely in the imagination and reflect all three of these meanings.

A scene designer says: "A few pages into a script and I begin to see places, or rather, bits and pieces of places. Sometimes it's the angle of a wall, sometimes a chair or a lamp. Sometimes I can feel humidity, or cold, and that's usually associated with a sense of color that might eventually become big, sweaty leaves or a row of tree skeletons against a white sky. The more I read, the more I see. Ultimately, what I see isn't nearly as important as the fact that I am seeing things, lots of things. Every time I sit down with a script I know something will be working up there. It's like having money in the bank."

"I have to put myself in a particular frame of mind, sometimes in a particular place, before I begin to feel what color and what shape my lights are

Figure 1–1. *A textural collage assembled by Keith Belli to visualize his response to early readings of* Antigone. *Photograph by Richard Ingham.*

going to take. It usually isn't when I'm reading the script, but afterwards. Most times it's after the set's already designed and in the shop. Sometimes it's when I'm watching rehearsal. Something happens that I react to. I've had it happen when I've been looking at a diagram of the theatre grid on my computer screen." The lighting designer searches for words. "What exactly do I see? Sure, it's an image. I see an image of the shape and color of light, and when I see it, the image tells me how to make it happen."

"I'm a hunter-gatherer," the costume designer explains. "I go through life collecting images of who people are and how and why they're dressed the way they are. I never get bored standing in line in the grocery store because I'm always storing up combinations of shirts and shoes and coats and dresses, and all the crazy things people do to their hair. As I get to know the characters in a play, I know I've probably got an image tucked away somewhere that will help bring the character to life. Sometimes it's as simple as the way I once saw somebody wear a baseball cap; sometimes it's

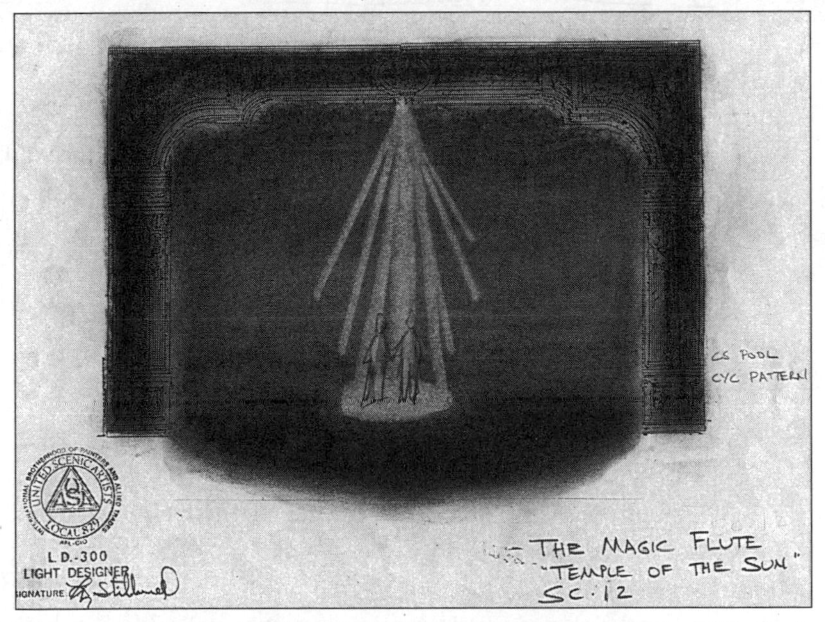

Figure 1–2. *An image created with light by Liz Stillwell for* The Magic Flute, *"Temple of the Sun," scene 12. Courtesy of Liz Stillwell.*

Figure 1–3. *Costumes details from a designer's image collection. From Arena Stage's production of* Stand-Up Tragedy, *by Bill Cain. Costume design by Paul Tazewell. Photograph by Joan Marcus.*

> a whole outfit. Mostly, because so much of my work is period stuff, the images I see don't really relate to anything I've actually seen. And yet they do. Somehow."

In brief, here is what these designers have to say about their relationships with imagination.

- "I know something will be working up there."
- "I see an image of the shape and color of light."
- "The images I see don't really relate to anything I've actually seen. And yet they do. Somehow."

Our next step is to pose some essential questions about what the imagination is and how theatre designers relate to it.

What is imagination?

What is an image in the mind?

What is the relationship between imagination and image?

What is the relationship between imagination and image and the sensible (or sensed) world?

What is the nature of the relationship between me and my imagination?

> Can I talk to it?
>
> Can it talk to me?
>
> Can I teach it anything?
>
> Can it teach me anything?
>
> Can I deliberately and consciously "make" images?
>
> Can I deliberately and consciously "erase" images?
>
> Are images always pictures? Do they ever include words and/or other sensory perceptions?
>
> Is it possible to train, or educate, the imagination in order to make it more responsive, more dependable, and more focused?

We will be exploring these questions as we examine ways of reading and coming to know theatrical texts, and how we use what we know and learn to inform the mysterious process called design. Theatrical design usually begins with a text, and designing is, in large part, a function of imagination. The connections between the two, however, are elusive.

A Bucket of Knowing

Images are related to knowledge in several ways.

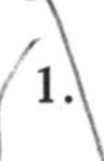

1. Images can underscore facts and experiences, making them seem more real and more true.

2. Images sometimes pop up out of the blue and solve knotty problems.

3. Images can be metaphors for things we already know, acting as different, or alternate, ways of knowing.

As we saw in Nathan's reaction to perceiving an image of falling, landing, and hurting, knowledge (in this case his grandmother's warning) can inform or incite an image, and an image (falling and being hurt) can inform or incite something we are in the process of knowing. When a fact or an understanding is accompanied by an image, we are doubly certain that what we know or understand is true. This is perhaps the mind's reiteration of the adage a picture is worth a thousand words.

Solving problems through images can be dramatic. These occurrences often involve solutions to problems that have defied ordinary tactics, such as rational thought, experimentation, and discussion. An image saves the day. Henri Poincaré, the nineteenth-century mathematician, described the circumstances that led up to the solution of a mathematical problem as follows: "One evening, contrary to my custom, I drank coffee and could not sleep. Ideas rose in crowds; I felt them collide until pairs interlocked, so to speak, making a stable combination which I experienced as a mental diagram."

Friedrich Kekulé, who originated the structure theory of organic chemistry, has been called "an intuitive genius." In the late nineteenth century, Kekulé saw an image of a circle in his mind, and recalling the idea that the forces coming from the atom are distributed geometrically, like the points of a tetrahedron, he conceived the molecular structure for benzene.

Albert Einstein appears to have been able to put his images to work on demand. In a letter to Jacques Hadamard, Einstein wrote: "The words or the language, as they are written or spoken, do not seem to play any role in my mechanism of thought. The psychical entities which seem to serve as elements in thought are certain signs and more or less clear images which can be 'voluntarily' reproduced and combined."

A metaphoric image operates much the same way metaphor does in language. It is a kind of poetic double, an implied comparison, in which two things are identified with each other in such a way that the metaphor means the original. These lines from W. H. Auden's poem "As I Walked Out One Evening" provide a good example.

As I walked out one evening,
  Walking down Bristol Street,
The crowds upon the pavement
  Were fields of harvest wheat.

Several years ago, I imagined a visual metaphor for what I know. It appeared on my personal image screen (which I fancy is located somewhere behind my eyes and midway between my ears). When I reconstruct this image, I see a bucket. It is a galvanized tin milk bucket just like the buckets I carried from the cow barn to the springhouse during childhood visits to my great-aunt's farm. This bucket sits on a flat stone under an old-fashioned pump spout. When it appears, it already contains several inches of original water. This water is what I came into the world knowing: my genetic material, the stuff passed on to me from all the humans who contributed to my essential humanity. Most people agree that humans inherit basic physical characteristics, like eye color and skin tone; many believe we also receive a variety of predispositions to react in certain ways to physical, mental, and emotional stimuli; and a few even maintain that through genetic inheritance, one generation is able to pass on ideas, opinions, and specific behaviors to the next. In other words, if you accepted all three possibilities, a banker's daughter could inherit her merchant banker parent's brown eyes and freckles, predisposition for gastric ulcers, talent for figures, and an inherent economic conservatism. Great controversy rages about what humans do and do not pass from generation to generation by way of genetic inheritance. The original water in my bucket rises above the controversy: it consists of all the stuff I got from those who went before me, whatever that stuff might be.

From the moment we are born, drops of knowing begin to drip from the pump spout into the bucket, each drop spreading out, or dispersing, throughout the water that is already there. The infant "learns" to suck, to see, to hear, to feel. The toddler crawls, walks, speaks, grasps, and explores. The child moves out into the world away from the family, storing up billions of new drops each year. Formal education, as well as experiences with art, literature, and music, add billions more. The drops keep coming for as long as a person lives.

Why the water-in-the-bucket image? Why not sand-in-a-bucket? If a bit of knowing was a grain of sand, it would always remain discrete, a unique grain of sand among many grains of sand. In my experience, bits of knowing are not discrete. The things we come to know do not merely add to what we already know; instead, they disperse throughout the entire bucket and constantly alter the composition of the whole.

The fact that new knowledge has the power to influence the ideas and opinions we already hold is one reason some people believe that knowledge is dangerous. A new experience of any sort can—and does—alter what I already know: like a drop of water dispersing throughout all the water in the bucket, its molecules bump into, set into motion, and rearrange, all the molecules that are already there. The attitudes already in the bucket get shaken up, turned around, reexamined, and sometimes changed.

The work of designers is intimately affected by experiences that mix up the stuff in their buckets. For example, a scene designer working on designs for a production of *King Lear* learns that his grandfather is suffering from Alzheimer's disease and has been placed in a nursing home. Shakespeare's text takes on new meaning because of the new information that dropped into the designer's life. His exploratory sketches are dark with looming shapes that cast angular shadows, perhaps reflecting his distress over his grandfather's condition and his fear that he will be badly treated.

An experience does not have to occur in the present to have an identical effect on the images that inform design work. A scene designer working on designs for *King Lear* might be reminded of his grandfather, who suffered from Alzheimer's disease and died in a nursing home ten, or twenty, years before. Perhaps the memory comes to him because he chanced upon a family photograph, or ran across a book his grandfather had given him. It is equally likely that the memory of his grandfather quite suddenly popped into his mind without seeming to be prompted by anything at all.

Indeed, an experience that causes a designer to know and see in a new way does not even have to be something that happened to that person, nor does it have to be something that actually occurred. Vivid experiences plop into our buckets by way of fiction as well as fact, through books, movies, paintings, articles in the newspaper, trips, chance conversations, what we hear on the radio, what our friends tell us, and indeed through every sort of human sensory encounter we can imagine.

Perception and Memory

> To note that the thing I call my individuality is only a pattern or dance, that is what it means when one discovers how long it takes for the atoms of the brain to be replaced by other atoms. The atoms come into my brain, dance a dance, and then go out—there are always new atoms, but always doing the same dance, remembering what the dance was yesterday.
>
> Richard P. Feynman, *"What Do You Care What Other People Think?"*

Theatre designers are people in whom the natural human propensity for noticing things, consciously, unconsciously, and through all the senses, is highly developed. Everything a designer senses and perceives throughout life influences the ideas and images from which designs are created. It is impossible to predict what sights, sounds, experiences, scents, tastes, or feelings will shape a designer's work.

Lighting designer Liz Stillwell describes an incident that illustrates how a strong visual image from her childhood influenced one of her recent designs.

> I have a great story about a dance I lit for Ballet Pacifica. It was about the Jews in America riding trains in the U.S. during World War II, while being aware of the Jews in Germany and the trains they were riding. The title is *Different Trains.* I had very strong images when I heard the music and saw the movement. I immediately sketched light shafts and round train headlights and geometric shapes. I also immediately felt the need for bare branch gobos and cold blue and white light for a feeling of black/white/gray.
>
> Later, after the concert, I was having dinner at my mother's and noticed a painting she had that used to hang in my room as a child. I was born in Germany on a military base and my parents bought the painting from a 13-year-old German girl. It is all shades of blue/gray with a cubistic sky, a bare tree, and a round cold moon. I realized all these images, colors, and textures were in my design of *Different Trains.* Germany to me is that painting and I hadn't been aware I had used it verbatim in my design.

Like Liz Stillwell, many theatre designers can recall at least one occasion in their professional lives when they were able to connect a design insight or decision with a specific event, separated in time and often in a vastly different context from the task at hand. In most cases, their awareness of the connection comes after the fact, and often, as in Liz Stillwell's case, seemingly by accident. Actually recognizing a specific connection, however, is the exception rather than the rule. Memory, like imagination, works in mysterious ways, its wonders to perform.

What Do We Remember?

My grandmother was a firm believer in the "universal storage" theory of memory. Whenever I was trying to remember some elusive fact, perhaps in preparation for a school quiz, she would reassure me: "Don't fret. When you

Figure 1–4. Two photographs from the Ballet Pacifica production of Different Trains. Notice the "headlights and paths of light" in the top photograph, and the gobo tree designs in the bottom photograph. Choreography by Molly Lynch. Photographs by Rick Lang.

learned it, it made a wrinkle in your brain. All you have to do is concentrate on finding the right wrinkle." Most of us want to believe that memory, located somewhere in the brain, is the warehouse in which everything we have ever experienced is stored. We may no longer associate memorable experiences with brain wrinkles, having adopted more scientific terms like neuron and synaptic connection, but we still hold onto the notion that all the sensory input from the world around us—the sights, sounds, and smells, and the more complex experiences that make up our lives—is stored in our brains. Forever.

Although many people believe the universal storage theory of memory, current scientific opinion does not support it. If, for example, we review the process by which our eyes record sight sensations and send them to the brain as perceptions, after which the brain interprets the perceptions, reacts to them, and finally files the whole experience in the appropriate part of our gray matter, we can see how impossible universal brain storage would be—and how wasteful.

Consider the number of visual sensations I experience during the twenty minutes it takes me to drive from my house to my office. Along the way, my eyes see all kinds of things: cars, drivers, trees, houses, bicycles, mailboxes, shops, bushes, and so on. I am aware that I see these things because I am conscious of them. In other words, sight perceptions have actually made it to my brain. During this same drive, however, my field of vision is open to dozens of other similar sights, which my eyes see but my brain does not register. Why does this happen? Why does my brain choose to see certain sight sensations and ignore others? What would it be like if all the objects within my field of vision were impressing their visual presences upon me while I was attempting to drive my car down the road? In the process of seeing everything, I would undoubtedly lose the ability to focus on anything, including the road, the lines marking the lanes, and the car ahead of me. I would more than likely end up crashing into a clearly visualized bush somewhere off to my right or left. In short, humans have the ability to negotiate their way through forests, over mountains, around traffic jams, and up and down hallways, shopping malls, and grocery store aisles, because our brains are programmed to ignore, or forget in advance, most of what we see. The result is focus, direction, and clarity of vision.

Each of us sees what his or her brain, in effect, chooses to see. It also appears that each brain chooses an ever so slightly different version of what there is to see. Therefore, when we speak of a visual artist as having a personal vision, we may well be referring to the biomechanics of a particular brain, rather than to the presence of a singular spiritual, or aesthetic, sensibility.

How much of what I consciously see, or focus upon, will I remember? Why can memory not grab every sight my brain perceives and store it away for future retrieval? Why, for example, can I not recall the license plate number of the car ahead of me on the road yesterday morning? I had forgotten the number moments after I turned off the road and into my parking lot. I can remember looking at the number; I can even recall thinking there was something unusual about the number. But I do not remember the number. I will never remember the number. The number is not present in my memory storage. Why? Was it because there was no reason to collect it? Because it was extraneous information? Or does my memory simply have an aversion to collecting numbers?

Unfortunately, there are no answers to these questions. Researchers do not know why we remember the particular things our brains choose to collect and file away for future use. Or why we forget others. There are, of course, certain kinds of experiences people in general tend to remember: traumatic events, momentous events, startling sights, and the hundreds of specifics that define each of our lives, from our social security number to the brand name of our favorite toothpaste. No one can explain, however, why one person remembers, in glaring detail, an ugly print that hung over the bed in a motel room she stayed in for two nights in 1990. Or why another person cannot remember even the smallest visual detail from the restaurant where his first meeting with his future wife took place.

Certainly the most disturbing thing about memory is its notorious unreliability. Not only do we not possess a record of all of our life experiences, the life experiences we remember may not be accurate. We may even recall detailed and specific memories of events that never occurred. Memory, it turns out, proves to be fertile ground for suggestibility, with lots of room for growing and changing.

Actually, if we take the knowledge bucket metaphor seriously, it is easy to understand why memory undergoes change. Whatever is stored in the brain changes because the brain itself changes. Memory is made up of two kinds of information: the original perception of the event, and information supplied after the perception of the event. It is impossible to predict how new perceptions will effect resident memories.

To complicate memory matters even further (and to bring us back into the theatre design ballpark), human brains are quite proficient at turning the memory of something that has merely been related to us (by another person, in a book, play, film, or on television) into something that we believe (remember) we have experienced. There is even a name for this phenomenon: cryptomnesia, which means remembering what someone has told you but forgetting that you have been told.

Many things about memory make it a frustrating part of our mental apparatus, particularly when we are trying to write clear answers to specific questions, or recall a telephone number only a moment after closing the directory. However, many of the frustrations with memory we experience in daily life are due to the very aspects of memory that contribute to our work as designers.

Earlier, I pointed out that theatre designers have a highly developed propensity for sensing, and for noticing, a vast assortment of things in the world around them. Theatre designers also have prodigiously acquisitive memories, strongly predisposed toward storing visual images and those miscellaneous facts that incite images. In her discussion of visual memory in *The World of the Imagination*, Eva Brann suggests that images may be stored in memory like slides loaded randomly in a carousel. Once recalled, the images themselves are clear and distinct. However, it is seldom possible to put a mental finger on a specific image at will. The best we can hope for is a mental meandering through random images, which, for theatre designers, is precisely how the unexpected, often exciting juxtaposition of images happens.

Design is often described as the combining of disparate elements into a coherent whole. In this endeavor, nothing is more useful to a designer than the capriciously selective memory, with its tendency to elaborate on reality and to engage in creative groupings.

Using Imagination

The Welsh poet Dylan Thomas once remarked that, as a young man, he wished his work to be "colossally original, like eggs laid by tigers." In his last work, *Under Milk Wood*, a verse drama for voices, Thomas drew on his own memory fragments to create a touching, humorous, memorable, and brilliantly original portrait of one day in the life of a Welsh village. Young theatre designers often waste a great deal of time searching for original visions, while ignoring the raw material for design that is already present within their own knowledge and experience. Designing for the theatre demands an active imagination, a keen sense of perception, and a fertile memory. All of us have the basic mental capacities; designers, knowingly and unknowingly, develop them.

Several months ago I asked some theatre designers to talk to me about their imaginations. I posed some of the questions listed at the beginning of this chapter. The following comments, drawn from these conversations, provide some excellent reflections on the various ways designers describe their relationship with their imaginations.

> I have learned to give my imagination time to work. After reading the script and seeing the set design and the beginnings of a costume design, I let my unconscious work when I am relaxed or asleep. Many times I will dream a design solution or awaken with an image that is the key to the lighting.

> My imagination is nonverbal and metaphoric. Words ruin the connection unless they are poetic.

> My imagination is pretty talkative. Mostly about the images. We (me and my imagination) have these conversations about what I'm seeing in my mind. Why red? I thought you decided no purple. Stuff like that.

> I can teach my imagination by observing other people's creative work in areas such as art, poetry, and film. I find it difficult to learn intuitively from the theatre work of other people because my left brain is watching too closely. When I sit in a theatre, I'm automatically at work taking notes on shutter cuts and cue timing.

> My imagination is triggered by the "What if?" question. What if I put a line right down the middle? What if one side was dark and one side was light? What if I painted a white circle on the dark side floor? What if the actors never stepped on the white circle? Images happen in my mind in response to the "What if's."

> Images come when I take walks, look at art books, read poetry.

> My best images are intruders. I hang out the flag early: Hey there, I'd like a little visual stuff for the third act. Then I do the routine: make up the bed, fix

breakfast, empty the pencil sharpener, you know. Bam. Right in the middle of pouring coffee. There it is. Angles. Color. My sister's garden. A cellar door. It's the only way.

My imagination improves with use and reflection. Practice keeps it in shape. The real skill is learning to listen to your imagination. An understanding of Jungian symbolism and mythology has helped me to interpret and better use my imagination.

I know this sounds crazy but I have this notion that my bulletin board is a reflection of my imagination. Every time I change the stuff on it—pretty often as you know—I think it's because my imagination is improving and I'll be able to make a better bulletin board. I probably rearrange my bulletin board every time I design a set.

I imagine myself walking around inside the play, saying the words, wearing . . . what? I sit down, get up, sit down again. I'm saying the same words. Suddenly I'm feeling a sleeve, tight at the wrist. The feeling always comes first. Then I begin to see it. I back off. The character stays. Now I can see the shape. There's no detail, but it's enough to draw.

Too little use of the imagination makes it more difficult to draw on, as if it gets hard like cold molasses and won't pour. My imagination is like rechargeable batteries. It recharges best if it's just been used up and loses its charge if left on the shelf too long. This is also how muscles work, get tired, rest, grow (when resting after being tired), and atrophy with disuse.

Plays 2

The dramatic critic must regard a script in terms of its performance potential. This means it cannot be treated as existing outside space and time . . . but rather as being embedded in them, as carrying spatial and temporal implications in its very fabric.

Richard Hornby, *Script into Performance*

In my hand I am holding a playscript. It is a brand new paperback copy of Pam Gems's play, *Stanley*. The covers are smooth and unmarked, the pages densely packed with all the corners intact. I look inside the back cover and notice that this playscript is 88 pages long. Inside the front cover I find six unnumbered pages, which contain: (1) a brief biographical sketch of playwright, Pam Gems; (2) a list of other playscripts from the publisher; (3) a title page; (4) the copyright and cautions page; (5) a list of the cast and artistic staff of the original production, which opened on February 1, 1996; and (6) a list of the characters in the play. Page 1 (implied because the first actual number to appear is a '2' on the following page) gets off to a familiar start: ACT 1, SCENE 1. A quick riffle through the still-crisp pages assures me that the words are arranged in a familiar spacial format, and distinguished by three typefaces. The character names, all flush with the left margin, are printed in capital letters. The dialogue, following the character names and continuing in indented blocks, appears in plain, lowercase type with appropriate capitals. The stage directions, sometimes preceding the segment of dialogue to which they refer and sometimes in separate, indented blocks, are all in italics. There is no doubt, I conclude. I am indeed holding a playscript. I may also conclude that I am not holding a novel, a work of nonfiction prose, or a poem. Generally speaking, one can recognize a playscript at first sight.

The differences between plays and other forms of writing are considerably more than skin deep, however. Plays read differently from novels. The strategies for finding reliable information in plays are not the same as those we use, for example, to gather facts from an article on continental drift. Very often, because there may be several characters in a play, each speaking from his or her own personal perspective, the facts the reader gathers are ambiguous and contradictory. It is sometimes more difficult to figure out who is telling the true story in a play than it is to separate truth from lies in speeches delivered by rival political candidates.

I have chosen to begin my exploration of the relationship between theatre designers and scripts by taking a close look at some of the differences between reading plays and reading other forms of writing. Most of these differences are obvious, indeed, they are so obvious that many readers tend to overlook them. Most readers, including those who work and study in the theatre, read far more narrative prose than dramatic writing in their daily lives. Like poetry, dramatic writing has its own forms for arranging words, and devices for communicating feelings and ideas. Reading a playscript requires a particular combination of awareness, attentiveness, and participation on the part of the reader. It is my hope that the following pages will help theatre designers develop this awareness and attentiveness, practice reading playscripts in a focused, active manner, and, in the process, become better collaborative partners. "I want the designers I work with to begin by talking to me about the play," Jon Jory, the producing director at Actors Theatre of Louisville, remarked recently. "I want, and need, to know what they've discovered in the script. Unfortunately, in my experience, most designers don't pay enough attention to the play and only want me to look at their research."

Plays, Prose, and Poetry

As children develop their reading skills in school, their focus is mainly on prose texts, particularly nonfiction prose. Although stories and poems make up the bulk of what is read to children, school-age readers need to learn the skills that make it possible for them to extract specific information from a variety of written materials and, through reading, to learn facts about many subjects. Many programs used to enhance reading skills feature short essays on subjects such as: "What Is Light?," "Are Snakes Slimy?," and "Ben

Franklin Flies a Kite." These reading experiences are followed by multiple-choice and fill-in-the-blank questions to test the young reader's comprehension of what he or she has just read. The child who is able to find correct answers in the words and phrases of informative prose paragraphs will soon be able to tackle a history textbook or an essay on rain forests.

Far too many reading teachers and reading textbooks continue to apply the process of reading for objective facts in nonfiction prose to reading prose fiction. Stories are followed by questions: Who is Jane? Who is Dick? What is the name of Jane and Dick's dog? List the most important things that happen in this story.

There is a constant emphasis, over many school years, on the written word as a simple conduit for factual information. This emphasis is responsible for considerable confusion, frustration, and irritation in older students who, in a high school literature class, suddenly find themselves face to face with a dense piece of imaginative prose fiction, such as William Faulkner's *The Sound and the Fury,* which does not lend itself to objective questions or straightforward answers. Prose fiction is often followed in the literature curriculum by poetry. Poems by Keats, Shelley, Yeats, or Eliot may be included, all of which are built on schemes of multiple meanings and ambiguities, rather than the straightforward delivery of information. By its very nature, poetry seems to mock the fact-finding reading skills so diligently acquired by young readers. Plays, which turn up only infrequently in general literature courses, are often the most challenging of all literary forms for the "prose-equals-information"–trained reader. Plays are deceptive. The sentences and paragraphs that appear to be informative prose are actually opinionated bits of dialogue spoken by many different voices. When plays are read for simple meaning, huge chunks appear to have little or no narrative coherence.

In certain ways, playscripts have more in common with poems than with prose. Both are constructed from a variety of components, such as line length, rhyme, stanza, sound, act, metaphor. Some of these structures are traditional and some are innovations in the work of a particular writer or group of writers. When we look at them in the most simplistic way possible, these structures are methods for choosing and assembling words in order to achieve a specific effect or meaning. The meaning of a poem or of a playscript is communicated both by the structure, or shape, of the piece, and by the words themselves. A reader receives the meaning of a Shakespearean sonnet, for example, by knowing what the words mean and by seeing where the words are located in the construct. Likewise, a play reveals its meaning not only through what the characters say but by where, when, why, and to whom they say it. An equation for reading a play, or a poem, might be:

words + structure + reader = meaning

Theatre designers are specialized readers who regularly read plays because they have been hired, or assigned, to create designs for a production and must find all the information (including inspiration) they need to inform their designs. In order to find these pieces of information, however, and to place them properly within the context of the play as a whole, designers have to learn to read playscripts with a clear understanding of exactly what a playscript is, how it is put together, and where and how to look for its most important clues. Because all of us have much more experience in reading novels and short stories than in reading plays, I will spend the next few pages examining some of the most significant differences between the ways prose fiction writers and playwrights tell their stories.

Reading Fiction Versus Reading Plays

Reading a play is very different from reading a novel or a short story. When I plunge into Jane Austen's *Northanger Abbey* or John Irving's *Son of the Circus*, or into a mystery novel by P. D. James, I enter a fictional universe which is complete within itself. I become a passive receiver of the words and, quite literally, leave the work of driving up to the author. I rely on prose passages to convey me from event to event, to describe scenes and characters, to comment on conversations between characters, and, overtly or subtly, to suggest what conclusions I should reach about the meaning of the novel or story.

Prose fiction writers drive their novels and stories by means of a narrative voice. The narrative voice in works of fiction appears in two main forms: the omniscient narrator and the first-person narrator. The omniscient narrator speaks in the third person and does not actively participate as a character in the action of the novel or story. Most fiction readers assume that the descriptive and expositional sections of such novels are being spoken by the author. The omniscient narrator is, therefore, a voice of considerable authority.

A first person narrator speaks with the voice of a character in the novel or short story. This involved narrator, speaking in the first person, usually participates in the action and narrates the story from the character's perspective. A first person narrator cannot "get into the head" of another character or objectively describe a scene if he or she was not present. First person narrators, therefore, do not have the same degree of authority displayed by omniscient narrators. However, since the author created the first person narrator to be his or her mouthpiece, most readers take it for granted that this character speaks for the author, that the first person narrator is merely an omniscient voice working under an assumed name.

A play, which is composed almost entirely of the direct speech of dramatic characters, each speaking from his or her individual perspective within a singular fictional reality and without the intervention of a narrative voice, presents an entirely different reading experience. In a play, who speaks for the author? Who makes sure all readers are following the same course of action? Who tells us what the characters are really thinking? Who tells us how to think about the characters and how to interpret the action? The simple answer is: no one. No single authoritative narrative voice exists in plays. Furthermore, because no such voice exists, a play reader who remains passive, waiting for an author/driver to describe the scene, point out the action, or illuminate the characters, will inevitably get lost along the way. It is up to the play reader to find, within the words the characters say, the details and the connections that reveal where the play takes place, who the characters are, and what happens. Although the fictional ingredients of a novel and a play are similar—an imagined world, characters, action—the mode of communication in a play demands much more active participation from the reader than a novel, or a short story.

I do not mean to suggest that reading a novel is necessarily easier than reading a play, although many people (including some theatre designers!) believe this to be the case. Many novels are extremely complex, multilayered entities that challenge the reader's knowledge, experience, and imagination. In general, however, a novel is complete within itself (even if it takes a dozen readings to uncover what is there), while a play is a carefully drafted, detailed plan for a complex production: the fully mounted theatrical event, complete with performers and audience. Plans, by nature and by design, require the reader to see and understand the finished product. The differences between reading a novel and reading a play are rather like the differences between walking around inside an actual building and reading the blueprint of that building. When I visit a friend's new house, I am more apt to appreciate its aesthetic qualities—the richness of its wood floors, the quality of light from its windows, the presence of a fireplace or a handsome stairway—than I am to focus on its underlying structure of struts and beams, or on the human thought processes that brought the house from ideas and images to reality. On the other hand, when I read a blueprint of a house, I have to become thoroughly engaged with the smallest detail of the graphically coded plan in order to see the potential structure it represents. I mentally collect and interpret symbols that tell me the size, shape, and arrangement of rooms, the access between rooms, and the location of doors, windows, and closets. Only after I have gathered a sufficient amount of information am I able to visualize the house from the plan. And, although certain practical skills, such as a knowledge of drafting symbols, measurements, scale, and proportion, are helpful to any reader of a blueprint, it is within my imagination that I ultimately translate the plan into the image of a house.

A play reader goes through a similar process, building the image of a whole fictional construct from the thousands of facts revealed in the dialogue of dramatic characters. When a playwright is particularly skillful at creating the ideas and images for a play *and* drafting it accurately, the play reader will be able to assimilate pieces of dramatic action and characterization and build a fictional, theatrical construct within his or her imagination. This close association playwrights have with building, constructing, and making is the reason why we name them playwrights rather than playwriters. There is no doubt that playwrights write, but they also build, make, shape, construct, arrange, rearrange, assemble, level, and even restore and renovate. Successful play readers are active participants who read the plan/playscript *and* imagine the play/production.

A costume designer contrasts his experiences reading Edith Wharton's *The House of Mirth* and Lillian Hellman's *Little Foxes*. The Wharton novel and the Hellman play are set at about the same time and share some similarity of theme:

> "I just got around to reading *The House of Mirth* last year. A friend gave me a copy for Christmas and I spent the whole week between Christmas and New Year's inside that world. The book dragged me in, held me there. I'd start reading and before I knew it two hours had gone by and it was a shock having to come back to family, food, and football games. I felt like I was living

in the book. At about the same time I was reading *The Little Foxes*, which I was going to design in February. I'd never read it before. I loved it. It excited me. I could hear actors speaking the lines. I combed their conversations for facts. I began to "see" what color dress Regina would have chosen, and why. I never "lost" myself; I was always alert. It was fun, sometimes exciting. It was not restful."

What Is Happening?

Prose fiction provides readers with much more information about what is going on in the story, and in many more direct ways, than playscripts. Consider the following examples:

> "First of all Alyosha went to see his father. As he approached the house, he remembered that the day before his father had insisted that he should enter it without being noticed by his brother Ivan. 'Why that?' Alyosha thought suddenly now. 'If father wants to tell something to me alone in secret, then why should I go in secret? I suppose in his excitement yesterday he wanted to say something else, but did not manage to,' he decided. He was nevertheless glad when Marfa, who opened the gate to him (Grigory, it seemed, was lying ill in the cottage), told him in reply to his question that Ivan had gone out two hours before." (Fyodor Dostoyevsky, *The Brothers Karamazov*, part 2, chapter 2)

In this passage from *The Brothers Karamazov*, the reader finds out where Alyosha is going and that he went there the day before. We hear him thinking about his father's behavior during yesterday's visit with regard to his brother, Ivan. In the second sentence, Alyosha approaches his destination. We find out who opens the door for him, who does not open the door for him and why, and that his brother is not at home.

Admittedly, this paragraph has more meaning for the reader who has read the entire book up to this point. Nevertheless, it is easy to figure out what is happening on the surface and to pick out the enormous number of facts Dostoyevsky has managed to pack into six sentences. Imagine trying to put all these actions and thoughts into a passage of dialogue!

As a contrast to the excerpt from *The Brothers Karamazov*, here is the dialogue from a short scene at the end of act 1 of David Hare's *Racing Demon*:

LIONEL: Tony. Tony.

TONY: It's you, Lionel.

LIONEL: You look like a ghost. I came in. I wanted . . . to ask you to dinner.

TONY: Dinner? That's very kind. But I can't. I've got . . . another invitation.

LIONEL: Really?

TONY: In town.

LIONEL: Oh yes?

TONY: I'm going to see . . . someone else.

LIONEL: Well, then, some other time.

TONY: Some other time, yes. Well, I must be going, or else I'll be late. Good to see you Lionel. I'll see you soon.

LIONEL: What can you do, Lord? You tell me. You show me the way. Go on. You explain why all this hurt has to come. Tell me. You understand everything. Why do the good always fight among themselves?

There is no narration or description in this passage, no narrative voice to tell the story, to reveal the thoughts of the characters, or to give any background for present action. Stage directions provide a few additional clues—the scene takes place in a church; Tony is on his knees throughout most of the scene; Tony exits before Lionel's final speech—but there is no storyteller/author's voice to guide the reader through what is actually happening, or what the characters are thinking during these moments in this fictional world. Outside the larger context of the play, this passage lacks even simple surface meaning. Reading these lines is a bit like being shown a fragment of a building blueprint, perhaps a section showing a small, rectangular space with two windows, a door, and what may be a closet or a pantry or perhaps an entryway to outside. Not only does the fragment tell the reader of the blueprint nothing much about the whole house, it says little or nothing definitive about the room itself.

What Is This Place?

Compare the ease with which a fiction writer is able to come right out and describe the house, the rooms, and the general atmosphere in which the characters live with the playwright's problem of inserting well-motivated descriptive details into pertinent and believable dialogue.

> As a house, Barton Cottage, though small, was comfortable and compact; but as a cottage it was defective, for the building was regular, the roof was tiled, the window shutters were not painted green, nor were the walls covered with honeysuckles. A narrow passage led directly through the house into the garden behind. On each side of the entrance was a sitting room about sixteen feet square, and beyond them were the offices and the stairs. Four bedrooms and two garrets formed the rest of the house. It had not been built many years and was in good repair. (Jane Austen, *Sense and Sensibility*, chapter 6)

This paragraph illustrates another example of a commonplace function of the descriptive narrative voice in novels that is not generally present in dramatic dialogue: the narrator not only presents an authoritative description of the scene, but also guides the reader toward an approved attitude about what is being described: Barton Cottage provides adequate shelter but it does not meet aesthetic expectations, which would have required an irregular floor plan, a tiled roof, green shutters, and a profusion of honeysuckle. Once again, consider the sheer amount of accessible information contained in this paragraph and try to imagine how you would convey it in a dramatic context using character-specific speech and dialogue appropriate to the dramatic situation.

There are a few playwrights who deliberately ignore the particulars of place and leave all such decisions to theatre designers. Most, however, work hard to slip descriptive clues into the mouths of their characters. This is a difficult, often frustrating task for the playwright, because descriptions of place in a dramatic dialogue must be appropriate to the action of the scene and to the nature of the character who is speaking. Place descriptions in plays do not come in nicely organized paragraphs; they pop up randomly and in a variety of contexts.

In Shakespeare's plays, stage directions are virtually nonexistent and those that appear in printed texts have often been added by later editors and stage managers. Because these plays were originally produced on an all but bare stage, Shakespeare became a master at inserting place descriptions into his dialogue, and thereby setting the scene. None of them seem arbitrary or extraneous because they invariably allow the character who delivers the lines to reveal a strong attitude about the place and tell the reader something about the character's own nature as well as the nature of the play.

KING [DUNCAN]: This castle hath a pleasant seat; the air
Nimbly and sweetly recommends itself
Unto our gentle senses.

BANQUO: This guest of summer,
The temple-haunting martlet, does approve
By his loved mansionry that the heaven's breath
Smells wooingly here. No jutty, frieze,
Buttress, nor coign of vantage, but this bird
Hath made his pendent bed and procreant cradle.
Where they most breed and haunt, I have observed
The air is delicate.

(*Macbeth*, act I, scene 6)

BOTTOM: Are we all met?

QUINCE: Pat, pat; and here's a marvailes convenient place for our rehearsal. This green plot shall be our stage, this hawthorn brake our tiring-house, and we will do it in action as we will do it before the Duke.

(*A Midsummer Night's Dream*, act III, scene 1)

Twentieth-century playwrights tackle the matter of place descriptions in a variety of ways, in general, using conversational strategies that do not violate action or character. Indeed, most modern playwrights contrive, like Shakespeare, to create dramatic dialogue in which the description of place also advances the action of the play, the development of a character or (and preferably) both.

PETER: Why did you come here? I had to chase all over town looking for you, only to finish up in this dump.

HELEN: Oh shut up! I've got a cold.

PETER: What on earth made you choose such a ghastly district?

HELEN: I can't afford to be so classy.

PETER: Tenements, cemetery, slaughterhouse.

HELEN: Oh we've got the lot here.

PETER: Nobody could live in a place like this.

JO: Only about fifty thousand people.

PETER: And a snotty-nosed daughter.

(Shelagh Delany, *A Taste of Honey*, act 1, scene 1)

VOICEOVER: They are concerned with interior decoration.

JERRY: So I'm tearing out that entire wall. Open all this up.

CATHY: Uh-huh.

JERRY: Then I buy good furniture.

CATHY: Uh-huh.

JERRY: I might take out that wall, too.

CATHY: Don't want to take out too many walls.

JERRY: Well, then, no more—just those two.

CATHY: Uh-huh.

(Constance Congdon, *Tales of the Lost Formicans*, act 1)

ALEX: What is that?

FANNY: Snow. Unless I miss my guess.

ALEX: Cold and wet on the tongue. Melts right off.

FANNY: Snow it is.

ALEX: Like no snow I've known before.

FANNY: A new snow. A strange snow. An unknown snow.

MARY: Lambent. Luminous.

ALEX: Snow from the moon, ladies!

FANNY: Yes!

MARY: Yes! Lunar snow is not annoying.

(Eric Overmyer, *On the Verge*, act 2)

Theatre designer/readers must become particularly adept at recognizing, interpreting, and seeing places through the eyes of characters speaking the dialogue of playscripts. Sometimes, as in Eugene O'Neill's *Long Day's Journey into Night*, different characters will describe the play's place differently, each from his or her own perspective. It becomes a fascinating design problem to figure out what the Tyrone summer house in New England is *really* like. Here are a few dialogue "clues":

MARY: His real estate bargains don't work out so well.

*

TYRONE: This house has been a home again.

*

MARY: I've never felt it was my home. It was wrong from the start. Everything was done in the cheapest way. Your father would never spend the money to make it right. It's just as well we haven't any friends here. I'd be ashamed to have them step in the door.

*

MARY: He's even proud of having this shabby place. He loves it here.

*

TYRONE: . . . I'm taxed to death.

*

EDMUND: Yes, on property worth a quarter of a million.

Consider the following questions—and the absence of simple, authoritative answers: What does James Tyrone "love" about his summer home? How shabby is "shabby"? Who are the friends Mary would be "ashamed" to have in the house? With what sort of house is Mary comparing this house? What is the real value of this piece of property? In the absence of a prose narrator to describe the property to us objectively, the reader/designer is forced to see the clues the playwright has drafted into the play's blueprint, to consider them individually and in context, and, eventually, to build the house and furnish it in his or her imagination. Because the clues about the true nature of the Tyrone summer home can be interpreted and assessed in different ways, general readers, and especially theatre designers, will imagine many different versions of the world in which *Long Day's Journey into Night* takes place. It is important to remember that if readers have been equally keen in recognizing and assessing the clues, no one image will be more *right* than any other. (We almost never call a theatre design *right* or *wrong*. A good design *works*; a poor one *doesn't work*. Right and wrong are absolutes and harken back to some authority, whereas working and not working suggest a range of possibilities and an ongoing process.)

Who Are These People?

Without an authorial voice to provide a reader/designer with the inside scoop on the motivations beneath what characters say, theatre designers, particularly

Figure 2–1. Three production photographs illustrating three different solutions to creating the Tyrone summer cottage on stage. The top photograph is from *Actors Theatre of Louisville*. The actors are Grant Sheehan, Gerald Harte, and Lenny Baker. The next is also from *Actors Theatre of Louisville*. The actors are Jean Inness, Tom Atkins, and Victor Jory. Both of these photographs are courtesy of *Actors Theatre of Louisville*. The photograph on p. 31 is from *Arena Stage*. The actors are Rainn Wilson and Richard Kneeland. Photograph by Joan Marcus.

Figure 2–1. Continued.

those responsible for creating the spaces in which characters live and the clothes they wear, must figure out ways to get inside the fictional heads of the characters through whose words, stories, descriptions, actions, and conflicts all plays are revealed. I like to think of this process as interviewing, or even having imaginary conversations with characters. But how, you may well ask, do living, breathing human readers manage to have conversations with purely fictional characters who exist only in plays?

As we have already seen with descriptions of place, in the case of James Tyrone's summer cottage, for example, the characters in a play view their world in very different ways. Designers cannot know what to believe about what a character says unless they know as much as possible about the nature of the character who is speaking. Like our interactions with fellow humans in daily life, we cannot begin to know the nature of a character in a play until we have gathered specific information about the character, usually through a combination of direct contact, observation, and other sources. Once we have enough information to feel that we understand the character, the next step is to examine this knowledge in relationship both to the world of the play, and to the way in which each of us understands human nature and expects human beings, including ourselves, to speak, think, and behave.

I approach the process of getting to know a character in active and personal terms—as a designer *talking to* a character—because this method emphasizes the importance of focusing on a unique entity, a specific fictional creation who is embodied only in the words of the playscript. The reader, whose human consciousness is constantly shifting, can raise a variety of issues and ask many different questions from many different points of view; the character, however, who exists entirely within the play, can respond only with the facts contained in the playscript. (If it occurs to you that confining your direct connection with a dramatic character to the text of the play in which that character appears will limit your design imagination, you can quickly dispel this concern by recalling the scores of text-based settings in which characters such as Hamlet, Volpone, Harlequin, Oedipus, Harpagon, and Medea have continued to come alive through many centuries of reexamination.)

But, you might object, this is character analysis, and is not character analysis the work of actors and directors? Costume designers often tell me that they rely on directors and, particularly in situations where a resident costume designer is working with a resident acting company, on individual actors to interpret the characters as they develop in the rehearsal process. Why should designers, who are already overworked, spend precious time getting to know characters, in a sense duplicating work already being done by others? My answer is simple: I believe a theatre production works best, and is most alive, when every member of the visual and performance team has connected individually and directly with the play's text, and has had his or her own conversations with the dramatic characters *as well as* with each other. In this way the production collaboration benefits from the insights of many attentive, active readers and the images of many imaginations.

In his book *The Dramatic Imagination*, the gifted and articulate theatre designer, Robert Edmond Jones, says, "The designer must learn to sense the atmosphere of the play with unusual clearness and exactness. He must actually live in it for a time, immerse himself in it, be baptized by it," and "the stage costume has an added significance in the theatre in that it is created to enhance the particular quality of a special occasion. It is designed for a particular character in a particular scene in a particular play—not just for a character in a scene in a play, but for *that* character, in *that* scene, in *that* play—and accordingly it is an organic and necessary part of the drama in which is appears."

How do we get to know "*that* character" in "*that* scene" in "*that* play"? Once again it is useful to compare the different ways in which readers get to know and understand characters in prose fiction and in playscripts. The following

Figure 2–2. *A costume obviously designed in Robert Edmond Jones's words, for "that character, in that scene, in that play." Craig Wallace as Jack Cade in* Henry VI *at The Shakespeare Theatre, Washington, D.C., adapted and directed by Michael Kahn. Photograph by Carol Rosegg.*

sentence, spoken by the novel's omniscient narrator, sums up David, a character in John Fowles's *The Ebony Tower*: "David was a young man who was above all tolerant, fair-minded and inquisitive." How would a playwright convey this information? (No, it is not enough for one character in a play to describe another character as "young, tolerant, fair-minded, and inquisitive." In a play, the opinion of one character is only that—one character's opinion—and carries no more authority than any other character's opinion.) Discovering the truth, or truths, about dramatic characters is very much like developing a general opinion about a new acquaintance, a co-worker, or a political candidate in everyday life. We accumulate information about the person, or character, by observing speech, specific actions, and general behavior. Some of the information we receive first-hand and some is reported to us. Willy Loman in Arthur Miller's *Death of a Salesman* is a modern American Everyman with a multifaceted, often contradictory nature. Here are a few clues to Willy Loman's character a reader can accumulate from the play's dialogue.

LINDA: But you're sixty years old. They can't expect you to keep traveling every week.

*

WILLY: If old man Wagner was alive I'd a been in charge of New York now!

*

WILLY: I'm fat. I'm very—foolish to look at, Linda.

*

LINDA: Willy, darling, you're the handsomest man in the world—

*

LINDA: Few men are idolized by their children the way you are.

*

THE WOMAN: You do make me laugh. It's good for me. And I think you're a wonderful man.

*

BIFF: [to Linda] He always, always wiped the floor with you. Never had an ounce of respect for you.

*

HAPPY: Well, let's face it: he's no hot-shot selling man. Except that sometimes, you have to admit it, he's a sweet personality.

*

CHARLIE: [to Willy]	When the hell are you going to grow up?
	*
BIFF: [to Willy]	You fake! You phony little fake! You fake!
	*
LINDA:	He was so wonderful with his hands.
	*
BIFF:	He had the wrong dreams. All, all, wrong.
	*
CHARLIE:	Willy was a salesman.

Willy Loman, the character, is all the above and more. In a successful collaboration, each of the dozens of choices theatre designers make as they work on a production of *Death of a Salesman*—Willy's shirts, shoes, and hat; his sample case; the troublesome refrigerator and the chairs in his kitchen; the location of his almost-paid-for house; and the lighting within its rooms—is grounded in everything the designers come to know and feel about Willy Loman through their careful attention to the play's dialogue. In a performance that works, the character's visual world, from the architecture of his house to the way he knots his tie, becomes inseparable from who he is.

Whether we are reading a playscript or getting to know a person in real life, we do not discover all there is to know in a single meeting. Only after many encounters, and considerable reflection, will a play reader be able to make as definite a statement about any character as "David was a young man who was above all tolerant, fair-minded, and inquisitive."

What Happened Before the Action Begins?

Prose fiction writers often begin stories with a version of the familiar "Once upon a time" spoken by an omniscient narrator, which allows them to tell readers simply and straightforwardly the facts they need to know to understand what is about to happen. In plays, background information, sometimes called "past circumstances," is the most difficult kind of material to weave into the dramatic dialogue taking place in the play's present and in real stage time. For the designer, it is important to know how to look for these facts and where, and to pinpoint the devices playwrights use to get this information across.

People who work in the theatre often make jokes about plays that open with a scene between the entirely peripheral maid and butler, who tell the

Figure 2–3. *Who is Willy Loman? From a production of* Death of a Salesman, *by Arthur Miller at Actors Theatre of Louisville. Actors are Eddie Jones, Lenka Peterson, James Eckhouse, and Steve Rankin. Photograph by David S. Talbott.*

audience, by way of a highly contrived conversation, that the master of the house is dying; the mistress is behaving strangely; the son has mysteriously disappeared; the daughter has eloped with the estate manager; and this morning a glass containing a mysterious substance was found by the master's physician on the master's bedside table. Although this revelatory tactic is stock-in-trade for mysteries and situation comedies on stage as well as on screen, it is also a time-honored theatrical convention that allows playwrights to insert background information early on with a minimum of fuss.

Shakespeare's opening scenes are often conversations between two or three characters that are chock-full of important facts on which subsequent action is built. In the opening thirty-five lines of act I, scene 1 of *King Lear*, for example, Kent, Gloucester, and Edmund reveal that

- The king is changing his mind about which of his sons-in-law he prefers and about the manner in which he plans to divide his kingdom, and it doesn't look as though he's going to make his choice on obvious grounds
- Gloucester has a "natural" son, Edmund, who, although technically illegitimate, is beloved of his father and appears "proper" to Kent
- Gloucester introduces Edmund to Kent, saying Kent is "my honorable friend"
- Kent expresses interest in Edmund
- Edmund seems to speak with modesty
- Edmund has been away for nine years and plans to leave again soon.

Although at first glance these thirty-five lines appear to contain disjointed, even random facts, each will prove to be an important background piece in the play's overall construct.

A first-person narrator, although somewhat less authoritative than the omniscient narrator, is potentially more engaging for the novel or short story reader because the voice is immediate and direct. Indeed, first-person exposition in prose fiction often reads a bit like dramatic dialogue. Compare the following to the lines in *King Lear*:

> "I remember drawing my mother. Born and raised in Crown Heights, her family high in the ranks of the Ladover aristocracy, she had gone through

> the Ladover school system for girls, and had married my father one week after her graduation from high school. She was nineteen when I was born and seemed more a sister to me than a mother." (Chaim Potok, *My Name Is Asher Lev*)

Modern playwrights sometimes create narrator characters who function in much the same way as first-person narrators do in prose fiction. In Athol Fugard's play *Valley Song*, a character named "the Author" "comes down and speaks directly to the audience." This character presents the personal history of another character, Buks, saying in part:

> He's planted a lot of pumpkin seeds in the course of his seventy-six years. And there's nothing haphazard about what he's doing either. When the young plants come up he wants to see them standing shoulder to shoulder in lines as straight as those the Sergeant Major drilled them into on the Sonderwater Parade Ground during the Second World War. Buks was a corporal in that famous old Coloured regiment, the Cape Corps, and was stationed up in the Transvaal guarding Italian Prisoners-of-War. He's in fact thinking about those days as he drops the seeds into the ground.

At the conclusion of this "narration," the Author sings a song, during the course of which "he moves into the character of Buks" and enters a scene with Buks's granddaughter, Veronica. Early in this first scene we learn more about Buks' past military career. Notice how the background information is presented in such a way that it also reveals something about the nature of the relationship between grandfather and granddaughter:

VERONICA: Tell me the truth, Oupa, were you a real soldier?

BUKS: What's a "real" soldier? I was just an ordinary soldier.

VERONICA: You know man, Oupa, like on TV. With a gun and all that.

BUKS: I had a gun. When I went on guard duty I had a real gun with real bullets . . . and all that.

VERONICA: But did you ever shoot anybody with it?

BUKS: No. I've told you before I was guarding Italian prisoners and none of them tried to escape.

VERONICA: Well then, you certainly didn't win the war, did you?

BUKS: No. I certainly didn't.

Sophocles and the other ancient Greek playwrights whose work survives created a kind of collective narrator in the Greek chorus. In Greek plays the chorus presents background facts to the audience, comments on the characters, and suggests ways in which present events might be interpreted in light of what has gone before. Because the chorus sections of Greek plays are often more difficult for modern readers to understand than the dialogue, it is particularly important for theatre designers to pay careful attention: What exactly is being revealed about past events and their effects on present action?

CHORAGOS: Seven captains at seven gates
Yielded their clanging arms to the god
That bends the battle-line and breaks it.
These two only, brothers in blood,
Face to face in matchless rage,
Mirroring each the other's death,
Clashed in long combat.

CHORUS: But now in the beautiful morning of victory
Let Thebes of the many chariots sing for joy!
With hearts for dancing we'll take leave of war:
Our temples shall be sweet with hymns of praise,
And the long night shall echo with our chorus.

CHORAGOS: But now at last our new King is coming:
Creon of Thebes, Menoikeus' son.
In this auspicious dawn of his reign
What are the new complexities
That shifting Fate has woven for him?
What is his counsel? Why has he summoned
The old men to hear him?

(Sophocles, *Antigone*, prologue, act 1)

In these lines the Choragos, or Chorus Leader, evokes a city newly emerged from battle, a battle in which brother fought against brother and each was slain by the other, "mirroring each other's death." These brothers were bitter enemies and faced each other with "matchless rage," and the battle, which ended in mutual death, was a "long combat." What does all this suggest about the physical state of the city? The Chorus claims that this is "the beautiful morning of victory" and celebration is in the air. Is it, indeed, a beautiful day? Are there signs of festivity, perhaps masking, or partially masking, the signs of war and death? Have the men of the chorus dressed for the occasion in which they will "take leave of war"? Despite the plans for "dancing" and "hymns of praise," there is uncertainty. A new king comes and, although this is "the auspicious dawn of his reign," he still has to contend with "shifting Fate." How will he look when he appears before the "old men" to offer "counsel"? Is this not the kind of careful, reflective playscript reading Robert Edmond Jones challenges us to undertake when he says, "The designer must learn to sense the atmosphere of the play with unusual clearness and exactness"?

Past circumstance and its effect on present action may also be revealed in a dramatic monologue spoken by one or more characters, either as an interior monologue or soliloquy (spoken thought), or as a narrative monologue (a story-within-a story). Hamlet's "To be, or not to be . . ." soliloquy in act 3, scene 1 of *Hamlet* is perhaps the best known example of spoken thought in all dramatic literature. However, Hamlet's interior monologue in act I, scene 2 has my vote as one of the most skillfully written examples in all dramatic literature of personal, intimate, and deeply felt emotion combined with sheer exposition. Indeed, the passage is so boldly informative that the reader must consciously be aware that the exposition comes from a single character and is decidedly biased. The passage begins with the line, "O, that this too too sullied flesh would melt," and goes on to describe events of the recent past within the royal house of Denmark:

- Hamlet's father is not long dead ("But two months dead, nay, not so much, not two").
- Hamlet's father was a good king ("So excellent a king") who loved his wife ("so loving to my mother").
- Hamlet's father is a god compared to his lecher uncle ("Hyperion to a satyr").
- Hamlet's mother loved his father ("Why, she would hang on him / As if increase of appetite had grown / By what it fed on") and yet she remarried with embarrassing haste ("within a month— / . . . —A little month").

- This marriage is, if not illegal, clearly immoral ("incestuous") and will not come to good ("It is not, nor it cannot come to good").

The passage ends with the intriguing statement that, no matter how he feels about these past events, Hamlet must remain silent ("But break my heart, for I must hold my tongue").

Where on the stage does Hamlet reveal this information? In stark light or in shadow? Sitting? Standing? On what? Is he dressed in black (his mother appears to indicate black clothing when she refers to his "nighted color," and Hamlet himself speaks of his "inky cloak," in his reply to Gertrude; on the other hand, both of them may be talking about the mood he projects rather than the color of his suit) or in some subtly jarring combination of colors that reflects his inner agitation? Is he disheveled and rumpled? Or scrupulously neat? Designers who listen carefully to what characters say, and ask searching questions of the characters and of themselves, discover visual answers.

Since the mid-twentieth century, playwrights have become increasingly fond of telling about past events in narrative monologues; on occasion, they have written whole acts, even whole plays, consisting entirely of dramatic narratives. Act 2, scene 1 of Nicky Silver's *Free Will and Wanton Lust* is a seven-page monologue by the character, Claire, in which she recounts a specific recent event in her life. In the course of telling that story, she branches out into several stories, which eventually form a network of memories that connects events in acts 1 and 3.

CLAIRE: I have, for a long time, been a person who tries to see the best in others. I have always tried to see the beauty in all things. No matter how grotesque. . . .

This morning I went to the dressmaker, to be fitted for a dress. I walked to the shop. It's not very far and I enjoy what's left of the fresh air. And I enjoy seeing people. Or I did. You see, more and more people seem to feel it alright to behave anyway they choose. For instance, more and more people seem to be—how shall I put this?—spitting. I don't approve of this. Sometimes they walk over to the curb and spit into the street, as if this were so much better than spitting in the middle of the pavement. It's not. It's just the same.

> And apparently not just men, but women too! With "hair-do's" and skirts. Now I want to see the beauty in all this but it's very hard. . . .

How Claire appears, what sort of world she inhabits, which chair she sits in, and what kind of fabric she allows to touch her skin are implicit in the text of this rich narrative monologue. Although no two designers will make precisely the same choices, the most workable and well-integrated choices will be incited by Claire's own words.

In Robert E. Ingham's play *Custer*, past events are present actions, and the narrative monologues, delivered by a Greek choruslike group of actors, are often indistinguishable from what we generally think of as dramatic dialogue.

FIRST MAN: In midafternoon of the 25th of June, 1876, five companies of the 7th Regiment of United States Regular cavalry, some two hundred and twenty men, with Lieutenant Colonel,

FIRST WOMAN: —and Brevet Major General—

FIRST MAN: George Armstrong Custer, found themselves quite suddenly to be surrounded by several thousand hostile Sioux and Cheyenne warriors, among the low hills and gullies East of the Little Big Horn River, in Southeastern Montana.

SECOND WOMAN: There were no survivors, and no one will ever know for sure how General Custer died, or what the nature of his "Last Stand" was.

FIRST WOMAN: He was—

FIRST MAN: —by reputation—

FIRST WOMAN: —the finest soldier on the Plains, and his the finest regiment, by repute.

SECOND WOMAN: And the mystery of his passing haunts us all.

In this poetic and ritualistic play, the reader collects story fragments and assembles them in several ways, each combination influenced by a particular character's point of view. Past events and present, onstage actions merge in a seamless theatrical event. In what sort of theatrical environment does this play exist? Although it is clearly historical, is it also real? How are the chorus characters related to the events they describe, particularly in light of the fact that there is a "mystery" in their story that "haunts us all." The answers, and the visual solutions, are inherent in the words of the play.

Worthy Readers

Robert Johnstone, a Shakespeare professor with a profound love for his subject, used to urge his students to become "worthy readers" of Shakespeare's plays. "Don't measure a great writer by the things that are easy for you to get from the play," he would say, in a conscious parody of the famous phrase from President John F. Kennedy's inaugural speech. "Measure yourselves by what you bring to the work."

All theatre designers have the potential to become worthy readers, not only of the works of Shakespeare but of the works of all serious and skillful playwrights. Designers are among the best equipped of all readers to recognize and understand the work of playwrights because playwrights are the builders of plays. The elements of design and the compositional strategies that inform how these elements combined to create visual coherence are closely related to the devices and strategies playwrights use to build and activate dramatic structures. Theatre designers, who constantly recognize and manipulate line and color, are singularly equipped to imagine the visual constructs inherent in dramatic blueprints and to bring the images in those blueprints to life. When theatre designers connect their special knowledge and experience to the work of reading playscripts, they become truly worthy readers.

Playscript Analysis 3

A man ought to read just as inclination leads him; for what he reads as a task will do him little good. A young man should read five hours in a day, and so may acquire a great deal of knowledge.

James Boswell, *The Life of Samuel Johnson*

The close details of a script should not be a cause of impatience, as is the case with far too many critics and theatre practitioners today, but rather a source of inspiration and delight.

Richard Hornby, *Script into Performance*

In the first half of the twentieth century, many houses had a room devoted to books and reading. It was called a library. Even in modest homes there was usually a reading place in the living room or parlor furnished with a comfortable chair and an adequate lamp. Today the home library has given way to the television room and the comfortable chair all too often faces the television set. Lamps are strategically placed so that light will not shine on the TV screen. In the television age, readers must forage for space and fend for themselves in the search for adequate light.

If the following tips for play readers preparing to read scripts seem excessively elementary and self-evident, pause for a moment and take a careful look at your own reading place and your own reading habits. Improvements may be in order.

Chairs, tables, and noise. Theatre designers spend a lot of time reading plays. Treat yourself to a comfortable reading chair (ideally, one that doesn't double for watching television) and a good lamp. Place a small table close by for your mug or glass and the pencil and pad you use for note taking. If you live in a house that occasionally passes for Grand Central Station, make a "do not disturb" sign and see that your companions take it seriously.

Atmosphere and aesthetics. Not many people can read effectively in the same room where talk shows or music videos fill the television screen. Design a reading space for yourself in a quiet area you find aesthetically pleasant, a place that works for you. Some readers prefer facing a window; others find the out-of-doors distracting and tuck themselves into a corner or a nook under a staircase. Consider bedrooms, porches, halls, and other out-of-the-way spots. If music helps you concentrate, place a speaker or a portable tape or CD player close by. Make a conscious decision that reading accessories, such as a footstool and a firm back pillow, are work-related tools, equal in importance to your electric pencil sharpener and templates. The place where you read and make connections with texts is as central to your design process as your desk and drawing board.

Single sitting. Organize your time so you can read a play in a single sitting. Because plays are so tightly packed with facts, both past and present, descriptive as well as active, it is difficult to keep all of them in your head if you let a day or even a few hours go by between acts. You can read straight through many contemporary plays in under two hours; Chekhov, Brecht, and Moliere require about three; Shakespeare, Jonson, and Aphra Behn close to four. Read each act without interruption; take an interval break between each act to freshen your coffee or tea and stretch your legs.

The First Time

Reading a play for the first time is never a smooth trip. Although we all begin to read with an expectation of what the journey will be like, the characters, ideas, and actions on the page soon overtake and outrun our assumptions. The reader is forever having to circle back to recall an earlier incident, and to take another look at it in light of what has just happened. A reader who has just learned a new fact about a particular character may be forced to pause for a moment to recall an earlier incident—"Aha," says the reader, "so that's why he was so eager to change the subject"—and quickly reinterprets what appears to have been true before. The more complicated the play, the more often the reader must shift perspectives in order to keep the whole work intact and in mind.

As we saw in chapter 2, individual bits of pertinent information are less obvious in a playscript and more apt to be scattered throughout the dialogue than in a novel or a short story, where a single paragraph can sum up a wealth of character analysis and background. Very few theatre designers, even the most observant, can collect enough details to begin the design process after a single reading. In the first reading, all readers, including theatre designers, simply turn each page in order to find out what happens next.

Even so, many designers insist that the first reading of a playscript informs their design process in important ways. Some designers make it a point to remember, even to record, the images produced by a first reading: a color, a shape, a piece of furniture, a quality of light. These initial images, even when they are vague and unfocused, and appear to have little apparent relevance to the play being read, assume an important role in a large number of designs. Some designers also pay careful attention to their emotional reactions after a first reading, knowing from experience that these responses will help them to make connections with audiences later on.

> I always pay attention to the way I feel after I read a play for the first time. I think that's the closest I'll ever come to what audiences experience when they see a production. Most of them only see it once, you know. Just once. We have to keep reminding ourselves that the audience only sees the play once; and we can't change that experience for them, no matter how many times we read it and how deeply we get inside its skin. No audience will ever get as much of the play as I've gotten by the time we get into tech rehearsals. That first reading is my only guide to the nature of the play's initial impact. If I come away with good feelings, I'll try to recreate those particular good feelings for the audience. If I come away with negative feelings, well, I'll try to make up for them somehow.

Other designers make the first reading as "neutral" as possible.

> I pretend I'm Joe Blow reading a play. I don't know nothing from plays. Never held a drawing pencil in my life. I just picked this script up. I'm reading it. That's all. Of course it's probably the most important part of my design process. How? Haven't a clue.

"But, I Don't Like the Play!"

Young designers with limited experience in reading playscripts often wonder how much weight they should give their personal opinion of a play after a first reading. Will they be able to create designs when their first reaction is some variation on "It was . . . okay." "Kind of boring, actually." "Very confusing." "Hard to understand." The most troubling response of all, of course, is: "I don't like it." "How," the young designer asks, "can I design anything good for a play I don't like?" A chorus of experienced designers quickly sings out that "liking is beside the point"; some designers even relate experiences in which they created their best and strongest designs for plays they thoroughly disliked, even hated, when they first read them. The skeptical young designer continues to glare at the offending playscript: "I just don't believe that's possible."

There are two reasons why liking or not liking a play after one reading (or several) is not necessarily a stumbling block on the path to successful design. One has to do with a basic human propensity, the other with the specific nature of playscripts (see chapter 2). Because these reasons also speak to a variety of less-than-positive responses to plays on the page, it is worthwhile to examine them briefly.

Humans are, in general, somewhat biased toward not liking, or not being comfortable with, new experiences. This knee-jerk-type response, stronger in some people than in others, may be the remnant of a survival strategy inherited from ancient ancestors and buried deep within the instinctive portion of our brains. Undoubtedly, there was a time in human history when eating an unfamiliar berry, trying to make friends with a strange creature, or wandering far from familiar paths could have signalled disaster for a single exceptionally adventuresome human, and for the group as a whole. In this modern, and thought-to-be safer world, most people still retain a built-in, initially negative response to new experiences. I can recall several foods that tasted awful the first time I put them in my mouth but which I subsequently came to relish; people I disliked on sight who later became good friends; and a great deal of music I found downright appalling when I first heard it but ultimately learned to love. Off the top of my head I can recall many plays I found boring, difficult, or needlessly demanding when I first read them and many others I simply did not like. In almost every case, once I began to interact with the characters and their dialogue, to look at the world of the play with a designer's eye, I became interested, then intrigued, and finally involved. In almost every case, involvement turned into an objective, informed liking. (Liking a play instinctively, and not being able to express why, can be as great an impediment to a successful design process as not liking a play.)

The second reason first-time readers may respond negatively to reading a play is that it is an incomplete experience. (Remember our discussion about the relationship between a playscript and a blueprint?) Readers must find and fill in parts of the story, pick up clues in the dialogue that explain present actions and past circumstances, and even figure out from scattered comments what the characters look like and where they are. This is tedious work. Getting good at it requires practice. It is no surprise that inexperienced readers of playscripts are much more apt to dislike a play after reading it the first time than people who read plays regularly, whether for business or for pleasure.

Therefore, my advice to the young designer who does not believe he or she can find enough inspiration in a particularly unlikable playscript to create spaces, orchestrate colors, or manipulate fabrics successfully is "Cool it." Read it again. Begin another conversation with the play and its characters. Listen better. Insofar as you can, reserve major judgments until after your next encounter.

The Second Time

The second reading of a novel, a short story, or a playscript is totally different from the first simply because the reader already knows what is going to happen. Some works of fiction do not need second readings. At the end of many books or stories, the reader comes to the end of the final page, sighs contentedly, and returns the volume to the shelf or hands it on to a friend. The reading has been a complete experience. By contrast, because a single reading of a playscript is always an incomplete experience, theatre designers know they must return to the script in order to find the facts that will inform their designs.

The Reader as Detective

It is impossible to describe the precise ways in which words in a script and the information they convey—the character traits, relationships, actions, places, times, and given circumstances that constitute a play—inform or incite a design. The transformation of dramatic writing into images of windows, chairs, waistcoats, collars, shafts of light and shadow is mysterious, personal, and probably biochemical. Neurons fire, synaptic connections are made, images appear. Someday neurochemists, neurophysiologists, and neurobiologists may understand the process, but even then, I doubt if the process itself will change dramatically.

A theatre designer collecting script facts proceeds very much like a crime-scene detective searching for physical clues and interviewing witnesses. After a good deal of examination and interpretation, the detective and his or her team will be able to construct a detailed re-creation of the crime. All investigative work requires patience. Playscript readers, like experienced detectives, do not jump to quick conclusions. They look, listen, collect, and remain objective. They are careful to classify information correctly and cautious about accepting the veracity of witnesses at face value. For a theatre designer reading a play in order to begin a design process, the second reading is often the start of the investigative phase that will result in some sort of structural script analysis.

Specific preparations for second readings are similar to those of detectives as they set out to investigate a crime. These include making careful provisions for recording information and/or taking notes. The usual tools are pencils, pens, notebooks, clipboards, typewriters, computers (laptop models are ideal), and recording devices. Whatever you use, make sure you are well supplied. (It must be admitted that some designers—unlike detectives who must write down everything so they will always be prepared to present concrete evidence in court—depend entirely upon their extraordinary memories to collect and classify script facts. Most of us, however, do not possess a memory of this caliber.)

In addition to launching the designer's script detective work, second readings often spark clear and specific visual images directly related to the script, which are the first building blocks from which the foundation for the design process is begun. As I examined my own script analysis process, I discovered that during second and third readings I pay special attention to exchanges of dialogue in which characters mention actual, tangible things. In his 1972 *Manifesto*, Richard Foreman says, "art is not concerned with essence / but with THING." He goes on to describe the purpose of art: "Create a ZONE in which placed things luminate." Because things illuminate scripts for me, I collect them assiduously while I read. Even things that will never physically appear on stage are often as important to me as the costume, chair, or candelabrum that does.

The following brief set of "thing-oriented" notes were made by a costume designer during and after three readings of Tony Kushner's *Angels in America*,

Part 1: Millenium Approaches. The notes refer to the dialogue in act 1, scene 4, the scene in which Prior tells Louis he has AIDS.

What happens? Louis & Prior talk after attending Louis' grandmother's funeral, before going to the cemetery. Prior is in a bad humor; his cat is missing; he blames Louis. Prior shows Louis a lesion on his arm; it is Kaposi's sarcoma. Prior says he is going to die. Prior wants Louis to go home with him. Louis leaves Prior "to go bury my grandma."

Louis' grandmother saw Emma Goldman speak; Emma Goldman wore a hat.

At the cemetery everyone will "put dirt on the coffin." "It's an old Jewish custom to express love." If you're late you don't get to.

Louis' grandmother reminded him of his mother; for that reason he didn't visit her.

Louis gets "closety" at family affairs; Prior says "You get butch."

Louis' grandmother's coffin was a "tiny little coffin."

Prior says Louis' cousin Doris is "a dyke."

Prior's cat might be long-haired: "Not a furball in sight."

Louis wanted a dog; named the cat "Little Sheba."

Louis says dogs have brains; Prior says cats have intuition.

Prior says he "did" a Shirley Booth: "floppy slippers, housecoat, curlers . . ." etc. "Come back, Little Sheba, come back."

Prior describes his lesion as "The wine-dark kiss of the angel of death."

LOUIS: Emma Goldman's hat, coffin and dirt, being late, mother/grandmother, Doris, dog.
PRIOR: watching people, watching Louis, cat, floppy slippers, housecoat, curlers, wine-dark lesion.

Subsequent Readings

Usually I read a play three times before I feel ready to talk to a director about designing it. Three times wasn't enough for Beckett. I read *Waiting for Godot* five times before I began to get a glimmer. Even then, it was only a glimmer. (Julie Hodge, scene designer)

When all the apparent facts have been gathered, a theatre designer's relationship with a playscript changes. By now, the designer has made notes about time and place, relationships and motivations, past happenings and future hopes. The questions that remain are What does it mean? How am I supposed to feel about what happens? What impact does the author mean the play to have on the audience? What impact do I expect the play to have on the audience? How will a production of this play "fit into" the current attitudes and beliefs of my audience and my community, and how will those same current attitudes and beliefs effect the production of this play?

After the third reading, but sometimes before, theatre designers will probably meet with the director and the other designers working on the production. At this point there is a strong temptation for designers to leave additional readings of the script up to the director and the actors in rehearsal while they turn their attention to researching visual information and begin to work at the drawing board.

Indeed, during the years when the director's vision, or "concept," was sacrosanct, theatre designers were not encouraged to concern themselves with exploring the play for meanings or make attempts to figure out how the production might affect an audience. Today, designers are taking a more active role in shaping the total production. Each collaboration begins with individual script work and expands into meetings with all members of the production group. The exchange of ideas, focusing on the playscript, continues during the designer's individual creative process and throughout the period when both the designs and the performances are being realized. Regular trips back into the playscript are as necessary for a designer as they are for the director and the performers, providing the common ground on which all the work is based.

General Script Analysis

> Play-analysis is of primary importance in the directing process. Merely feeling about a play is entirely insufficient. Play-analysis (structural analysis) must be mastered as a technique so that it can be used in approaching all aspects of the theatrical art in all plays, historical as well as modern. (Francis Hodge, *Play Directing*)

Once the designer has collected a sufficient number of playscript facts (what constitutes "sufficient" varies considerably from person to person), the next step is to organize them in a useful and informative way. Even if they do not think of it as a defined task, most theatre designers today engage in an organizing and classifying process that is usually referred to as playscript analysis. For some, it may be taking general and sporadic notes while reading or using transparent pens in different colors to highlight words and phrases directly on the pages of the script. For others, it is a careful study of the elements from which a particular play is made and may result in a dozen pages of well-organized notes and lists, possibly even a chart or two. No matter how casual or formal the approach is, doing playscript analysis is the designer's first dramatic action.

As I have suggested, my favorite analogy for the process of discovering and then organizing script facts is the meticulous investigation of a crime site. The investigating detectives note its contents and its inhabitants, interrogate witnesses, and consider all outside influences that have directly affected the event. Objectivity is important to both processes, as well as the discipline to look first and assign a context later. "Just give me the facts ma'am," the TV detective Sergeant Joe Friday used to instruct crime witnesses on the popular television series *Dragnet*. I often find myself saying the same words to young designers who are learning to read scripts: "Just give me the facts." Of course, theatre designers must have faith, just as detectives do, that "the facts," discovered and individually noted, will eventually form patterns from which detailed images of actions emerge. They can then interpret these patterns to create an accurate, or truthful, structure.

It is at this point that the analogy between solving crimes and making theatre loses its usefulness. An explanation of why the analogy fails will help us to understand how a group of trained theatre people, sometimes strangers to each other when the work begins, are able, as a group, to create a successful, focused theatrical event. In the criminal investigation, the structure of the crime as pieced together from everything the detectives collect, hear, and observe is tested in a courtroom. There, it is subjected to at least one opposing interpretation. By the time all the witnesses and attorneys have finished examining the original structure, that structure may have come to look quite different. One version of the crime will prevail and the accused will be pronounced guilty or innocent. In this courtroom model, one version of the facts, one interpretation of the events, wins out over all others.

Good theatre is never a matter of winning. Good theatre is collaborative. Winning or losing is not an issue; guilt or innocence is not a consideration; judging does not happen. Ideally, a theatre production comes into being in an informal, nonconfrontational setting where the designers and a director sit around a table, discuss their individual responses to the script, and eventually come to a commonly perceived idea and image structure of the play.

The director's role in today's theatrical collaborations is one of leadership. A modern director brings practical information to the table (performance place and dates, rehearsal schedule, budgets, potential casting, and so on), as well as a point of view about production style and performance theory. The director may, although not always, have a particular passion for bringing a specific script to life on the stage. The best directors hear and see the idea structures of their design colleagues and are able to find connections between them. As the discussions progress, these directors guide and shape the various collaborative efforts into coherence.

Playwright, Not Playwriter

As I noted in chapter 2, the word *playwright* gives us our first clue about the nature of a playscript. A *wright* is "a constructive workman," an "artificer," a "maker." The word *playwright* carries the sense that the play's author does not merely write a script but builds a plan with an edifice-to-come in mind. A novelist, for example, can create a lavishly described scene, set in a vast castle, peopled by hundreds of characters, horses, and a herd of sheep, featuring a public execution described in vivid, bloody detail. A playwright, contemplating a dramatization of the same scene, must always remain aware of the restrictions imposed by performance spaces and live actors, the myriad problems associated with having animals on the stage, and the technical difficulties (as well as considerations of taste) involved in staging a graphic execution in front of a live audience.

Playwrights make plays about any and every subject or character, draw on an infinite number of themes, and compose actions of all kinds. These subjects, characters, themes, and actions, however, must be shaped and built into a structure that will meet the specific dramatic needs of a play. There are hundreds of variations on the play structure, but all plays, from Greek tragedy through Restoration comedy and modern realism, share significant similarities: plays are written to be performed; all plays are performed within a defined space; characters, imitated by actors, act out the story; the action occurs in the present, in real time; the interaction of the audience affects every performance.

Playscript analysis is the process of discovering the unique structure within a single play. The person doing this kind of analysis must understand a play's components in order to find and examine how the playwright has shaped and manipulated his or her vision to meet the needs, and fit within the confines, of the basic construction model.

Formal Script Analysis

The most common scheme for playscript analysis appears to have been popularized by Francis Hodge in *Play Directing*, first published in 1971. Using the six components of drama outlined by Aristotle in his *Poetics* as a foundation, Hodge defines "seven major areas of play-analysis" as:

1. given circumstances;
2. dialogue;
3. dramatic action;
4. characters;
5. idea;
6. tempos;
7. moods.

These "major areas" are a group of classifications into which script facts can be organized and analyzed.

Why would a theatre designer want to spend time and effort on making a formal script analysis? Can it be at all practical? Consider the following analogy: Suppose someone assigned you to take a walk in the woods, and when you returned asked you to describe in detail everything you saw. You would certainly return with impressions and feelings but, when you began your description you would have a hard time recalling specifics. If, on the other hand, you were given a targeted assignment—look carefully at trees and rocks and for signs of mammals, for example—you would return quite able to describe leaf shapes, to compare rock sizes and colors, and to discuss the probable identity of the mammal that left identifiable tracks along the path. We already know that we perceive and remember, in part, through categorization. By deciding what general areas you are going to explore before you begin, you increase the probability of success in your search. "Read that script and be able to talk about everything that's in it" is a daunting assignment for theatre designers, but that is what we face without a plan. Conversely, "Read this script and separate the facts as they fall into the following seven (or six, or eight) categories" makes sense to our brains and is therefore both a reasonable and a rewarding task.

Using a formal method of script analysis is not a new idea, nor is it restricted to a single writer. Two of the most recent books on the subject on my shelf, *Script Analysis: Reading and Understanding the Playscript for Production*, by David Grote; and *Script Analysis for Actors, Directors, and Designers*, by James Thomas, both focus the analytical search on categories very similar to those outlined by Hodge in *Play Directing*. The "Outline for Playscript Analysis" in chapter 1 of Ingham and Covey's *The Costume Designer's Handbook* was also influenced by Hodge, although the categories are labeled and organized differently and have increased in number from seven to nine.

An Outline for Playscript Analysis

The following playscript analysis outline is the one I currently use and share with my students. It changes in small ways from year to year because I regularly revise and, hopefully, improve it. This outline has been constructed as a series of questions. Not all of these questions will apply to every script you read and examine, and some scripts may require you to create additional questions. Answer the questions that do apply as concisely and as specifically as possible. Note script references and record page numbers on your outline so you can locate your references quickly.

I. WHERE ARE THEY?

a. *In what country, city, place, building, room, etc.?*

b. *How do the characters describe the place they are in?*

c. *Is there any special significance to the place they are in?*

II. WHEN ARE THEY?

a. *In what day, month, year, century, season, time of day, etc.?*

b. *Do the characters have anything specific to say about when they are?*

c. *Is there any special significance to when they are? Is it, for instance, a national holiday?*

III. WHO ARE THEY? (Consider characters separately and as a group or groups.)

a. *How are they related?*

b. *What are their roles in life? Include jobs and professions as well as social and economic classes.*

c. *What do they think of each other?*

d. *What do they think of themselves?*

e. *Under what form of government do they live? What are their attitudes about the form of government under which they live?*

f. *What role does religion play in their lives? Which religion? What are their attitudes about their religion?*

g. *What are the prevailing attitudes toward sex, family, marriage, and ethical conduct? Do they live within or rebel against these attitudes?*

IV. WHAT HAPPENED BEFORE THE PLAY BEGAN?

Limit your facts to information given in the dialogue but be sure to "listen" carefully; much of what you discover will come from casual clues, which can occur in a variety of contexts.

V. WHAT IS THE FUNCTION OF EACH CHARACTER IN THE PLAY?

a. *Principal characters:*

Who is the protagonist?

Note primary action(s)

Who is the antagonist?

Note primary action(s)

What are the functions of the other principal characters?

b. *Secondary characters:*

What is the function of each?

c. *Crowds and functionaries:*

Note functions

VI. WHAT KINDS OF DIALOGUE DO THE CHARACTERS SPEAK?

a. *Realistic?*

b. *Naturalistic?*

c. *Literary?*

d. *Poetry?*

e. *Other?*

VII. WHAT HAPPENS IN THE PLAY?

a. *Briefly describe the principal event in the play.*

b. *Construct an action chart for the play.*

VIII. WHAT IS THE PLAY'S THEME?

This will only become apparent when you have read the script several times, and perhaps not until rehearsals are well underway.

Working Through the Playscript Analysis Outline

The first time you start to work through a detailed playscript outline for a moderately complicated play, it will seem enormously time-consuming. But careful reading and attention to detail take time and a good deal of persistence. A fully completed outline may be many pages in length. However, if you continue to use the same basic format, the steps involved become more routine and less formidable each time you go through the process. As you become more familiar with the elements from which plays are made, you also pick up clues in the playscript and perceive the play's structure more quickly. Your first few playscript analyses may require ten to twenty hours of reading, rereading, searching, and recording. However, an experienced theatre designer who has been offered a script to design early one afternoon, and is expected to attend an initial production meeting the next morning at nine o'clock sharp, can prepare a creditable script analysis in four or five hours and still get a good night's sleep.

There is nothing magic about the order of the outline and very little that is orderly about the process itself. When I first began to do systematic playscript analysis as part of my design process, I simply jotted down clue notes, one after the other, on legal pads. After I had finished collecting as many facts as I could find in two or three readings, I cut the individual notes apart, organized them into categories, and stapled or glued them onto sheets of notebook paper, which I kept in a binder. Later, I experimented with several colors of highlighter pens, which I used to mark clues in the script itself, transferring only general information to my own notes. Now I keep a copy of the script analysis outline saved as an open document in my computer (a Macintosh PowerBook). For each script I work on, I copy the outline and fill it in. I insert bits of image-provoking information as I discover them in the text and continue to add, subtract, question, correct, and organize facts and observations in what is very much like a conversation, carried out on the computer screen, between me and the play.

Exploring the Categories

Here are some examples of ways you can use the playscript analysis questions to focus your reading on specific words, phrases, and exchanges in the dialogue. The words contain clues that provide answers to the questions. For designers, the words to which you respond must also incite visual pictures or images. The examples are drawn from several different plays; if this or any other approach to playscript analysis is going to be useful, it must work with a wide variety of scripts, whether past or present. The script passages within each example have been gathered from an entire playscript, an act or scene, or a single short section in the play. I have not connected these examples with specific images because no two designers will see the same chair, dress, color, texture, shadow, or lamp.

I. WHERE ARE THEY?

a. *In what country, city, place, building, room, etc.?*

b. *How do the characters describe the place they are in?*

c. *Is there any special significance to the place they are in?*

Cloud Nine, *by Caryl Churchill (from act 1):*

CLIVE: . . . though far from home . . .
We serve the queen wherever we may roam,

*

Figure 3–1. *A very specific place! From* Middle-Aged White Guys, *by Jane Martin at Actors Theatre of Louisville, with Leo Burmester and Karen Grassle. Photograph by Richard Trigg.*

CLIVE: Long ride in the bush.

*

CLIVE: We are not in this country to enjoy ourselves.

*

BETTY: We're not in this country to enjoy ourselves.

*

CLIVE: Ah what a haven of peace to come home to. The cool, the calm, the beauty.

*

BETTY: I had left my book inside on the piano. I was in the hammock.

*

CLIVE: Isn't that Harry riding down the hill?

*

BETTY: Sometimes the sunset is so terrifying I can't bear to look.

*

CLIVE: Elsewhere in the empire the sun is rising.

*

BETTY: Harry looks so small on the hillside.

*

CLIVE:	Edward will go home to school shortly.
	*
HARRY:	Built a raft and went up the river . . . They have a lot of skulls around the place but not white men's I think . . . If I should die in this forsaken spot . . .
	*
CLIVE:	You are dark like this continent. Mysterious, treacherous . . . when I lifted the mosquito netting . . .
	*
MRS. SAUNDERS:	I do like living in your house where there's plenty of guns.
	*
ELLEN:	I am going to lock you in the nursery until suppertime.
	*
CLIVE:	The heat of the day has gone . . . cool drinks in the gazebo . . .
	*
HARRY:	Where can I go except into the jungle to hide?
	*
CLIVE:	You have been away from England too long.

On page 4 of the *Cloud Nine* acting edition, below the cast list, is the following statement: ACT I—Africa, 1880. Clues gathered from the act 1 dialogue begin to flesh out some of the particulars of place. The family is *far from home.* Beyond the house in which they live (*where there's plenty of guns*), there is *jungle*, a *river*, a *hillside*, and Clive returns home from a *long ride in the bush*. Clive describes *this continent* (and Mrs. Saunders!) as *dark*, *mysterious*, and *treacherous*. Betty says *the sunset is so terrifying I can't bear to look*. And yet, surrounded by an African wilderness, the family home is furnished with a piano, a hammock, a nursery, and a gazebo. Betty reads a book; the nanny, Ellen, threatens to lock young Edward up in the nursery; and Clive describes his home as a *haven of peace*. A sense of duty keeps them in Africa; possibly the same sense of duty compels them to try to live as if they were in England. *We serve the queen wherever we may roam*, sings Clive. Betty and Clive remind each other: *We are not in this country to enjoy ourselves.* And yet, wild Africa has wormed its way into their very British world.

II. WHEN ARE THEY?

a. *In what day, month, year, century, season, time of day, etc.?*

b. *Do the characters have anything specific to say about when they are?*

c. *Is there any special significance to when they are? Is it, for instance, a national holiday?*

Figure 3–2. *A portrait of the family in act 1 of Caryl Churchill's* Cloud Nine, *in costumes which help place them in a specific time period. From a production at Arena Stage, Washington, D.C. Photograph by Joan Marcus.*

Cat on a Hot Tin Roof, *by Tennessee Williams:*

MARGARET: I tell you I got so nervous at that table tonight . . .

*

MARGARET: And the no-neck monsters were ranged around the table, some in high chairs and some on th' *Books of Knowledge*, all in fancy little paper caps in honor of Big Daddy's birthday . . .

*

BRICK: What party?

MARGARET: Big Daddy's birthday party.

BRICK: Is this Big Daddy's birthday?

MARGARET: You know this is Big Daddy's birthday.

BRICK: No, I don't. I forgot it.

*

BIG MAMA: We just got the full report from the laboratory at the Ochsner Clinic, completely negative, son, ev'rything negative, right on down the line!

*

MARGARET: But tonight they're going to tell her the truth about it. When Big Daddy goes to bed, they're going to tell her that he is dying of cancer.

*

MARGARET: . . . this is Big Daddy's last birthday.

*

MARGARET: . . . he broke his ankle last night jumping hurdles on the high school athletic field!

*

MAE: I wonder if the mosquitoes are active tonight?

*

BIG DADDY: I still have desire for women and this is my sixty-fifth birthday.

*

MAE: You're eight years older'n Brick . . .

*

MAE: Why, Gooper has given himself body and soul to keeping this place up for the past five years since Big Daddy's health started failing.

*

MAE: . . . Still a football player at twenty-seven!

*

BIG MAMA: Time goes by so fast. Nothin' can outrun it. Death commences too early—almost before you're half acquainted with life—you meet the other.

It is night and the time of year when *mosquitoes* may be *active*. The night is special in several ways: *this is Big Daddy's birthday* and a celebration is in progress with children (*the no-neck monsters*) *ranged around the table . . . all in fancy little paper caps*. On this birthday night, Big Daddy is sixty-five years old and still has *desire for women*. The night is special for Big Mama who *just got the full report* on Big Daddy's health and was told that his tests were *completely negative*. Before this special night is over, however, Big Mama will be told *the truth*: that Big Daddy is *dying of cancer*. The night before this special night, Brick broke his ankle *jumping hurdles on the high school athletic fields*. Brick is *still a football player at twenty-seven*. Brick says he does not remember it is Big Daddy's birthday. *I forgot it*. Gooper, who is *eight years older'n Brick*, dedicates himself to *keeping this place up* and, by inference, is not immature and does not go around pretending to be an athlete. It is diffi-

(a)

(b)

Figure 3–3. *Six production photographs that suggest the power of visual images in the communication of character through the visual production. (a)* Getting Out *at Actors Theatre of Louisville with Lynn Cohen and Susan Kingsley. Photograph by David S. Talbott. (b)* Blithe Spirit *at Arena Stage with Ellen Karas and Sarah Marshall. Photograph by Stan Barouh. (c) Act 2 of* Cloud Nine *at Mary Washington College with Jeremiah Patterson, Tiffany Hayzlett, and Emily Hilton. Photograph by David Hunt. (d)* Holiday Heart *at Arena Stage with Donna Biscoe, Afi McClendon, and Jeffery V. Thompson. Photograph by Stan Barouh. (e)* Henry V *at The Shakespeare Theatre, Washington, D.C., with Vivienne Benesch, Ted Van Griethuysen, and Harry Hamlin. Photograph by Carol Rosegg. (f)* The Taming of the Shrew *at The Shakespeare Theatre, Washington, D.C., with Jonathan Epstein and Any van Nostrand. Photograph by Carol Pratt.*

cult to imagine how a single night can portend so much anguish. There are shadows in every corner. *This is Big Daddy's last birthday. Death commences too early.*

III. WHO ARE THEY?

(Consider characters separately and as a group or groups.)

a. *How are they related?*

Getting Out, *by Marsha Norman:*

MOTHER: June's havin another baby. Don't know when to quit, that girl.
Course, I ain't one to talk.

ARLENE: Have you seen Joey?

MOTHER: An Ray . . .
Ray ain't had a day of luck in his life.
Least bein locked up now, he'll keep off June til the baby gits here.

(c)

(d)

Figure 3–3. *Continued*

ARLENE:	Have you seen Joey?
MOTHER:	Your daddy ain't doin' too good right now. Man's been dying for ten years, to hear him tell it. You'd think he'd git tired of it and jus go ahead . . . pass on.
ARLENE:	Mother . . .

(e)

(f)

Figure 3–3. *Continued*

MOTHER: Yeah, I seen 'im. Bout two years ago. Got your stringy hair.

ARLENE: You got a picture?

MOTHER: You was right to give him up. Foster homes is good for some kids.

ARLENE: How'd you see him?

MOTHER: I was down at Detention Center pickin up Pete.

ARLENE: How is he?

MOTHER:	I could be workin at the Detention Center I been there so much. All I gotta do's have somethin big goin on and I git a call to come after one of you. Can't jus have kids, no, gotta be pickin em up all over town.
ARLENE:	You was just tellin me . . .
MOTHER:	Pete is taller, that's all.
ARLENE:	You was just tellin me how you saw Joey.
MOTHER:	I'm comin back in the cab an I seen him waitin for the bus.
ARLENE:	What'd he say?
MOTHER:	Oh, I didn't stop. If the kid don't even know you, Arlie, he sure ain't gonna know who I am.
ARLENE:	How come he couldn't stay at Shirley's?
MOTHER:	Cause Shirley never was crazy about washin more diapers. She's the only smart kid I got. Anyway, social worker only put him there til she could find him a foster home.

Mother is mother; Arlene is daughter. What about the rest of the gang?

1. June (Arlene's sister?), pregnant. Joey?
2. Ray, father of June's baby; *locked up now.* Joey?
3. Arlene's daddy, *ain't doin' too good right now.* Joey? *stringy hair; You was right to give him up. Foster homes is good for some kids.*
4. Pete (Arlene's brother?) at the Detention Center. *Pete is taller.* Joey? *waitin for the bus. don't know you.*
5. Shirley (Arlene's sister?) could not keep Joey *cause Shirley never was crazy about washin more diapers. She's the only smart kid I got.*

This exchange comes close to being a parody of a normal mother and daughter exchanging family news and gossip after a long separation. It is a terrible exchange; it is also more than a little funny.

b. *What are their roles in life?* Include jobs and professions as well as social and economic status.

The Shadow Box, *by Michael Cristofer:*

Exchanges (act I) from the characters who have been assigned to Cottage One: Joe, Maggie, and Steve.

JOE: My family is coming today.

VOICE OF THE INTERVIEWER:
Yes. We know.

JOE: It's been a long time. Almost six months. They would have come sooner, but we couldn't afford it. Not after all these goddamn bills.

*

JOE: Maggie always wanted a place in the mountains.

*

STEVE: So many goddamn trees . . . Bunk beds and a fireplace . . . We got any wood?

*

STEVE: I'll show you the guitar. It was pretty cheap.

*

MAGGIE: How do I look? It's a new dress.

JOE: You look real pretty.

MAGGIE: I got dressed for the plane. I don't know. I should have worn pants. You get so tired, sitting, all pushed together like that.

*

MAGGIE: . . . Oh, yeah. I made a ham . . . .

JOE: What?

MAGGIE: A ham. We can have it for lunch.

JOE: Christ!

MAGGIE: What's the matter? It's no good?

JOE: You mean you carried a ham three thousand miles across the country?

MAGGIE: No. I put it under the seat.

*

STEVE: We never did get our farm. We should do that. We should get that farm.

JOE: Well, maybe we should have.

MAGGIE: Don't start on the farm, for God's sake. It always ends up bad when you start on the farm.

*

JOE:	Fifty weeks a year in a flat-wire shop. Twenty-four years.
	*
MAGGIE:	We had the saloon in between. And the oil truck . . .
JOE:	A bartender and a truck driver in between.

Maggie is not used to airplanes. She was uncomfortable traveling in a narrow seat wearing *a new dress*. She brought a home-cooked ham *three thousand miles across the country*; she put it *under the seat*. Steve is eager to show his father his guitar, which *was pretty cheap*. Joe worked in the same shop for *twenty-four years*. This is a working-class family who has had hopes and dreams. One of those dreams was for *a place in the mountains*; the other was for a farm. It is ironic that the place to which Joe has come to die is in the mountains. Steve points out that the place has *so many goddamn trees* and *a fireplace*.

c. *What do they think of themselves?*

d. *What do they think of each other?*

Romeo and Juliet (*act 1, scene 4*):

ROMEO:	Give me a torch. I am not for this ambling; Being but heavy, I will bear the light.
MERCUTIO:	Nay, gentle Romeo, we must have you dance.
ROMEO:	Not I, believe me. You have dancing shoes With nimble soles; I have a soul of lead So stakes me to the ground I cannot move.
MERCUTIO:	You are a lover. Borrow Cupid's wings And soar with them above a common bound.
ROMEO:	I am too sore enpierced with his shaft To soar with his light feathers, and so bound I cannot bound a pitch above dull woe. Under love's heavy burden do I sink.

There are clues in this passage that prompt a designer to see the difference between Romeo's and Mercutio's appearance as they go to the Capulet party: each one comments on how he sees himself and on how he sees the other. Mercutio wants Romeo to put on an outward show; Mercutio appears to have adopted an outward show. Mercutio is dressed for *ambling* and wears, at least metaphorically speaking, *dancing shoes* and *nimble soles*. Romeo is *heavy* and has *a soul of lead*. He definitely does not want to take Mercutio's advice to wear *light feathers* or to *Borrow Cupid's wings*. It is difficult to believe that Romeo is thoughtless in his dress, however, because he wants to be sure others will see his *dull woe*. Here are two rich kids: one ostentatiously showing off his lovesick state; the other merely showing off.

e. *Under what form of government do they live?* What are their attitudes about the form of government under which they live?

Macbeth (*act 2, scene 3*):

MACDUFF: Confusion now hath made his masterpiece
Most sacrilegious murder hath broke ope
The Lord's anointed temple, and stole thence
The life o' th' building

MACBETH: What is 't you say? The life?

LENNOX: Mean you his Majesty?

MACDUFF: Approach the chamber, and destroy your sight
With a new Gorgon: do not bid me speak;
See, and then speak yourselves. Awake, awake!
Ring the alarum bell. Murder and Treason!
Banquo and Donalbain! Malcolm! Awake!
Shake off this downy sleep, death's counterfeit,
And look on death itself! Up, up, and see
The great doom's image!

The murder of King Duncan is no ordinary murder. It is *sacrilegious*, against divine law as well as human law. The *Lord's anointed temple*, the divinely inspired seat of rule, has been murdered, not merely the man. A murder of this sort threatens the whole country, *The life o' th' building*, and is as terrible an event as the end of the world, *The great doom*. When Macbeth kills Duncan he is committing *Murder, Treason*, and sacrilege. Macbeth's act does not take on its proper significance if we do not focus on the place of the monarchy in the world of this play.

The struggle for power is being played out on the highest possible spiritual plane within the human imagination. Macbeth puts his own soul, as well as the soul of his country in the gravest possible danger when he kills a king.

f. *What role does religion play in their lives?* Which religion? What are their attitudes about their religion?

Henry V (from act 2, scene 2):

KING: Arrest them to the answer of the law
And God acquit them of their practices!

*

SCROOP: Our purposes God justly hath discovered,
And I repent my fault more than my death—

CAMBRIDGE: But God be thanked for prevention,
Which I in sufferance heartily will rejoice,
Beseeching God, and you, to pardon me.

*

GREY: Never did faithful subject more rejoice
At the discovery of most dangerous treason
Than I do at this hour joy o'er myself,
Prevented from a damned enterprise.
My fault, but not my body, pardon, Sovereign.

*

KING: Now, lords, for France; the enterprise whereof
Shall be to you as us, like glorious.
We doubt not of a fair and lucky war,
Since God so graciously hath brought to light
This dangerous treason, lurking in our way
To hinder our beginnings. We doubt not now
But every rub is smoothed on our way.
Then, forth, dear countrymen. Let us deliver
Our puissance into the hand of God,
Putting it straight in expedition.
Cheerly to sea; the signs of war advance:
No king of England, if not King of France.

It is easy to imagine that the Christian God is present and active in this scene. Henry and the traitors all acknowledge God's direct influence on the events at hand. According to Henry, God *brought to light / This dangerous treason*. Scroop gives God credit for having *discovered* the plot, and Cambridge thanks God for *prevention* of the plot's success. Grey admits that the enterprise was *damned* from the outset. Henry reads the discovery of *This dangerous treason* as a sign from God that the *enterprise* they are undertaking [seizing the French crown!] will be *fair and lucky*. As in all dealings with God, however, faith is paramount, and they must *deliver / Our puissance into the hand of God*. Even though their path is *smoothed*, every obstacle removed, and they will set off *Cheerly to sea*, there is still a bargain pending: Henry will only know he is England's true king when, submitting his forces to *the hand of God*, he achieves *King of France*.

g. *What are the prevailing attitudes toward sex, family, marriage, and ethical conduct?* Do they live within or rebel against these attitudes?

Long Day's Journey into Night, *by Eugene O'Neill*:

Outwardly, the behavior of all four members of this complex family is consistent with the prevailing attitudes of their decade. The play takes place in 1912. Within each character, however, there is enormous tension between the ideal and the actual, and between the many levels or layers of behavior. While analyzing this play, it is interesting to consider the ways in which memories are altered by subsequent events and how skillfully the playwright uses this all-too-human mental strategy to create these multidimensional characters.

When we are reading *Long Day's Journey into Night*, it is hard to know whom to believe. One of the great traps inherent in drawing images from this play is becoming sidetracked by trying to figure out who is telling the truth. Try, instead, to collect facts in as objective a way as possible, paying no attention to the contradictions that appear in almost every exchange. Categorize the conflicting statements into parallel realities. Include pertinent evidence given by all characters. In discovering Mary's parallel realities, consider the following:

1. Mary at the convent school
2. Mary's relationships with her mother and father
3. Mary's meeting with, and marriage to, James Tyrone
4. The life of an actor's wife
5. Motherhood

6. Drug addiction
7. The present day and night

The following sections of dialogue contain some of the many facts that illuminate Mary as a wife, a mother, and a religious person.

MARY [to the maid, Cathleen]: I fell in love right then. So did he, he told me afterwards. I forgot all about becoming a nun or a concert pianist. All I wanted was to be his wife. Thirty-six years ago, but I can see it as clearly as if it were tonight! We've loved each other ever since. And in all those thirty-six years, there has never been a breath of scandal about him. I mean, with any other woman. Never since he met me. That has made me very happy, Cathleen. It has made me forgive so many other things.

*

MARY: But I must confess, James, although I couldn't help loving you, I would never have married you if I'd known you drank so much. I remember the first night your barroom friends had to help you up to the door of our hotel room, and knocked and then ran away before I came to the door. We were still on our honeymoon, do you remember?

TYRONE: I don't remember! It wasn't on our honeymoon! And I never in my life had to be helped to bed, or missed a performance!

*

MARY: She [Mary's mother] didn't approve of my marrying—especially an actor. I think she hoped I would become a nun. She used to scold my father. She'd grumble, "You never tell me, never mind what it costs, when I buy anything! You've spoiled that girl so, I pity her husband if she ever marries. She'll expect him to give her the moon. She'll never make a good wife."
Poor Mother.

But she was mistaken, wasn't she, James? I haven't been such a bad wife, have I?

TYRONE: I'm not complaining, Mary.

MARY: At least, I've loved you dearly, and done the best I could—under the circumstances.

*

MARY [to herself]: I hope, sometime, without meaning it, I will take an overdose. I never could do it deliberately. The Blessed Virgin would never forgive me, then.

*

TYRONE [to Edmund]: And the idea she might have become a nun. That's the worst. Your mother was one of the most beautiful girls you could ever see. She knew it, too. She was a bit of a rogue and a coquette, God bless her, behind all her shyness and blushes. She was never made to renounce the world. She was bursting with health and high spirits and the love of loving.

*

EDMUND [to Tyrone]: You've dragged her around on the road, season after season, on one-night stands, with no one she could talk to, waiting night after night in dirty hotel rooms for you to come with a bun on after the bars closed! Christ, is it any wonder she didn't want to be cured. Jesus, when I think of it I hate your guts!

*

MARY [from final speech]: . . . I told her I wanted to be a nun. I explained how sure I was of my vocation, that I had prayed to the Blessed Virgin to make me sure, and to find me worthy. I told Mother I had a true vision . . . that the Blessed Virgin had smiled and blessed me with her consent. But Mother Elizabeth told me I must be more sure than that, even, that I must prove it wasn't simply my imagination. She said, if I was so sure, then I wouldn't mind putting myself to a test by going home after I graduated, and living as other girls

> lived, going out to parties and dances and enjoying myself; . . . I was shocked . . . I knew it was simply a waste of time. After I left her, I felt all mixed up, so I went to the shrine and prayed to the Blessed Virgin and found peace again because I knew she heard my prayer and would always love me and see no harm ever came to me so long as I never lost my faith in her. That was in the winter of senior year. Then in the spring something happened to me. Yes, I remember. I fell in love with James Tyrone and was so happy for a time.

IV. WHAT HAPPENED BEFORE THE PLAY BEGAN?

In chapter 2, beginning on page 18, I addressed several of the strategies playwrights use to insert information about past events into present action. Becoming aware of these strategies will help you know how and where to look for what happened before the play began.

Sometimes, the revelation of a past event or events may also add a bit of suspense to the present action. What happened? When? Where? Why? Wait, tell me more! For reasons I cannot explain, visualizing certain past events in the lives of dramatic characters often allows me to see them in sudden, sharp detail.

In Marsha Norman's *Getting Out*, Arlene has just been released from prison and returned to her hometown of Louisville, Kentucky. The event, or events, that precipitated a change in her former behavior and led to her parole are revealed throughout the play in a confusion of seemingly random details; they only become coherent when the pieces are fully assembled in the final scenes. Here are a few of the dialogue facts that lead up to the revelation Arlene is finally able to make.

WARDEN'S VOICE: . . . Subject now considered completely rehabilitated.

*

BENNIE: You ain't as strong as you was.

ARLENE: I ain't as mean as I was.

*

BENNIE: Listen, ever prison in Alabama's usin' plastic forks now on account of what you done.

*

Figure 3–4. *The story of what has happened to these women is pieced together throughout the action in Steve Gooch's* Female Transport. *From the production at Actors Theatre of Louisville with Adale O'Brien, Patricia Pearcy, Mary Ed Porter, and Susan Kingsley. Photograph courtesy of Actors Theatre of Louisville.*

ARLENE:	*(Pulls a cheaply framed picture of Jesus out of the trunk.)* Chaplain give me this.
BENNIE:	He got it for free, I bet.
ARLENE:	Now, look here. That chaplain was good to me, so you can shut up about him.
BENNIE:	Fine. Fine.

*

MOTHER:	So, you're callin' yourself Arlene, now?
ARLENE:	Yes.
MOTHER:	Don't want your girlie name no more?
ARLENE:	Somethin like that.
MOTHER:	They call you Arlene in prison?
ARLENE:	Not at first when I was being hateful. Just my number then.
MOTHER:	You always been hateful.
ARLENE:	There was this chaplain, he called me Arlene from the first day he come to talk to me.

*

ARLENE:	I ain't Arlie.
BENNIE:	No, I guess you ain't.
ARLENE:	Arlie coulda killed you.

*

RUBY:	You don't seem like Candy said.
ARLENE:	She tell you I was a killer?
RUBY:	More like the meanest bitch that ever walked. I seen lots worse than you.
ARLENE:	I been lots worse.

V. WHAT IS THE FUNCTION OF EACH CHARACTER IN THE PLAY?

Always remember that a play is a skillfully wrought structure constructed by a playwright. The job of the structure is to communicate a specific story in order to affect an audience in as many predictable ways as possible (given that audiences are a notoriously unpredictable lot!). Playwrights consciously create characters to carry out the actions of the play and to communicate its meaning. Dramatic characters have well-defined jobs to do. An important part of every designer's playscript analysis process is to examine each character to determine what function, or functions, the playwright expects that character to fulfill. Seeing the characters in terms of the jobs they perform allows designers to successfully create and manipulate visual focus on the stage.

a. *Principal characters:*
Who is the protagonist?
Note primary action(s)

Every play is activated by a character who wants something insistently enough to keep the action going until the story is told. We call this character the protagonist, "the chief personage in a drama." If you have difficulty identifying the protagonist in a play, turn your search around and look for the character without whose presence the play could not move forward. Protagonists are generally quite outspoken in proclaiming what they want. Spend a few moments thinking about how familiar protagonists such as Mother Courage, Hamlet, Hedda Gabbler, Willie Loman, Blanche duBois, or Tartuffe function within their respective structures. What similarities do you find between the ways they move toward achieving their goals?

Getting Out, *by Marsha Norman:*

Arlene is the protagonist of *Getting Out*. Her fifth line in the play is: "Look, I'm gonna do all right. I done all right before Pine Ridge, an I done all right at Pine Ridge. An I'm gonna do all right here."

In spite of all she faces in the course of the play's action, Arlene holds fast to her determination to *do all right*. She rejects Carl's proposal to go back to work for him as a prostitute. She refuses to let Bennie take care of her. She goes out to the store and buys groceries. She allows Ruby to become a friend. And, most important of all, she begins to come to terms with her past.

Who is the antagonist?
Note primary action(s)

Arlie, Arlene's *girlie name* self, provides the insistent parade of obstacles Arlene faces as she struggles to *do all right*. Arlie, the antagonist, is all the past events that are vividly alive in the present and threaten to overpower Arlene's desire to change her life. Arlie's primary action is to constantly remind Arlene of every painful, angry, degrading, vicious thing she ever did. Because I'm still here, Arlie seems to say, you'll never change; you'll never *do all right*.

What are the functions of the other principal characters?

Mother is the negative portrait of a maternal figure.

MOTHER: I woulda wrote you but I didn't have nuthin to say. An no money to send, so what's the use?

ARLENE: I made out.

Carl was all she had in the past: lover, father to her child, pimp, leech. As the only love she has ever known, he is her greatest danger in the present.

ARLENE: Can't trust anybody.

RUBY: Well, you don't want to trust him, that's for sure.

ARLENE: We spent a lot of time together, me an Carl.

RUBY: He live here?

ARLENE: No, he jus broke outta Bricktown near where I was. I got word there sayin he'd meet me. I didn't believe it then, but he don't lie, Carl don't.

RUBY: You thinkin of goin with him?

ARLENE: They'll catch him. I told him but he don't listen.

RUBY: Funny ain't it, the number a' men come without ears.

Bennie is a father figure; he is old enough to be her father. He was a prison guard and the only one who could, or would, interact with Arlie. He has left his guard's job (unbeknownst to her) in order to drive her from Alabama to Louisville. He expects to remain with her. He loves her in his fashion: as something to care for, an intriguing challenge in an otherwise dull life, youth, and sex. Who knows how formidable an obstacle he might have presented to the new Arlene if he had not tried to force sex on her. He does. He loses.

BENNIE: Well, look. Least you can take my number at the motel and give me a ring if you need something. Here, I wrote it down for you. . . .

ARLENE: O.K. then. I got your number.

Ruby is the upstairs neighbor. She is the role model, an ex-con who is out of jail and working, but whose life is not particularly appealing. Ruby is reality.

ARLENE: . . . I can't git no work that will pay good cause I can't do nuthin. It'll be years fore I have a nice rug for this place. I'll never even have some ol Ford to drive around, I'll never take Joey to no fair . . . I'll have to wear this fuckin dress for the rest of my life. What kind of life is that?

RUBY: It's outside.

b. *Secondary characters:*
What is the function of each?

School Principal: Arlie is too much trouble for an overworked administrator. Besides, who wants to get involved with the possibility of incest?

SCHOOL PRINCIPAL: . . . I have four hundred other children to take care of here and what have I been doing? Breaking up your fights, talking to your truant officer and washing your writing off the bathroom wall. Well, I've had enough. . . .

Warden: Represents the rational world. Attempts to deal with Arlie in ways that make her more irrational.

WARDEN: Arlie, you see the other girls on the dorm walking around, free to do whatever they want? If we felt the way you seem to think we do, everyone would be in lockup. When you get out of segregation, you can go to the records office and have your time explained to you.

ARLIE: It won't make no sense.

Doctor: Wants to help. Does not have the knowledge or understanding to help. Tries. Never makes a dent.

DOCTOR: What's this about Cindy?

ARLIE: She told Mr. Dawson some lies about me.

DOCTOR: I bet.

ARLIE: She said I fuck my Daddy for money.

DOCTOR: And what did you do when she said that?

ARLIE: What do you think I did? I beat the shit out of her.

DOCTOR: And that's a good way to work out your problem?

ARLIE: She ain't done it since.

DOCTOR: She's been in traction since.

c. *Crowds and functionaries:*
Note functions

The *guards*, with the exception of Bennie, torment Arlie and feed her anger. When she explodes, they punish and confine her.

VI. WHAT KINDS OF DIALOGUE DO THE CHARACTERS SPEAK?

a. *Naturalistic?*

b. *Realistic?*

c. *Literary?*

d. *Poetry?*

c. *Other?*

Rarely, if ever, are conversations in real life made up of words chosen only to facilitate specific actions and communicate predetermined intentions. Dramatic dialogue, on the other hand, is always a carefully crafted imitation of actual speech, even when the exchanges seem to be completely natural.

When the playwright employs regional accents, the halting speech of inarticulate characters, or the broken speech of a character under great emotional duress, we call it *naturalistic dialogue*. The dialogue in *Getting Out* is naturalistic.

BENNIE: Wish I had a kid. Life ain't, well, complete, without no kids to play ball with an take fishin. Dorrie, though, she had them backaches an that neuralgia, day I married her to the day she died. Good woman though. No drinkin, no card playin, real sweet voice. . . . what was that song she used to sing? . . . Oh, yeah. . . .

Realistic dialogue might be described as an extremely fluent version of actual speech. The characters speak in complete sentences and prose paragraphs. They express themselves clearly and may use words and grammatical constructions we seldom encounter in conversation. The plays of Ibsen, Chekhov, and Shaw are all written in realistic dialogue, as is *Long Day's Journey into Night*.

MARY: Good heavens, how down in the mouth you look, Jamie. What's the matter now?

JAMIE: Nothing.

MARY: Oh, I'd forgotten you've been working on the front hedge. That accounts for your sinking into the dumps, doesn't it?

JAMIE: If you want to think so, Mama.

MARY: Well, that's the effect it always has, isn't it? What a big baby you are! Isn't he, Edmund?

EDMUND: He's certainly a fool to care what anyone thinks.

Literary dialogue is an even more heightened version of speech that contains few, if any, colloquialisms or slang phrases. Literary dialogue is prose employing colorful language devices, sometimes including metaphor and simile. Speeches are neat, concise, and well balanced. English Restoration comedy abounds with literary dialogue, such as this exchange from Richard Brinsley Sheridan's *School for Scandal*.

SIR BENJAMIN: To say truth, ma'am, 'tis very vulgar to print; and, as my little productions are mostly satires and lampoons on particular people, I find they circulate more by giving copies in confidence to the friends of the parties—however, I have some love elegies, which, when favored with this lady's smiles, I mean to give to the public.

CRABTREE: 'Fore heav'n, ma'am, they'll immortalize you!—you'll be handed down to posterity like Petrarch's Laura, or Waller's Sacharissa.

SIR BENJAMIN: Yes, Madam, I think you will like them, when you shall see them on a beautiful quarto page, where a neat rivulet of text shall murmur through a meadow of margin. 'Fore gad, they will be the most elegant things of their kind!

The language of the theatre has been poetry for a much longer period of time than it has been prose. In the late sixteenth century, playwrights, including Shakespeare, began to combine prose and poetry in dialogue, usually assigning poetry to the upper classes and prose to characters of less genteel birth. An interesting turnabout of this custom occurs in *Henry V* (act 2, scene 1), when Pistol descends into verse to lambast Nym.

PISTOL: "Solus," egregious dog? O viper vile!
The "solus" in thy most marvelous face!
The "solus" in thy teeth, and in thy throat,
And in thy hateful lungs, yea, in thy maw, perdy!
And, which is worse, within thy nasty mouth!
I do retort the "solus" in thy bowels;
For I can take, and Pistol's cock is up,
And flashing fire will follow.

VII. WHAT HAPPENS IN THE PLAY?

a. *Briefly describe the principal event in the play.*

For example, in *Romeo and Juliet*, Shakespeare describes two families, the Montagues and the Capulets, who are at war with each other. Romeo, a Montague, and Juliet, a Capulet, fall in love and marry in secret. Unfortunately, Juliet's father has promised her to someone else. When she refuses to marry her father's choice, he tells her to get married, or leave his house. Juliet asks Friar Laurence for advice and he gives her a poison that makes her seem dead for "two and forty hours." Romeo fails to get the message that Juliet's seeming death is only a temporary sleep, so when he finds Juliet, he believes she is actually dead. Romeo kills himself. Juliet wakes, sees Romeo dead and kills herself. After the lovers are dead, the Montague family and the Capulet family declare peace.

b. Construct an action chart for the play.

An action chart has both practical and aesthetic functions. Practically, it shows the designers which characters will be on the stage in any one scene, or section, of the play. The chart is an invaluable aid in planning costume and

Romeo & Juliet	I-1	I-2	I-3	I-4	I-5	II-1	II-2	II-3	II-4	II-5	II-6	III-1
Chorus	X											
Escalus-Prince	X											X
Paris		X										
Montague	X											X
Capulet	X	X			X							X
Romeo	X	X		X	X	X	X	X	X		X	X
Mercutio				X	X	X			X			X
Benvolio	X	X		X	X	X			X			X
Tybalt	X				X							X
Friar Laurence								X			X	
Friar John												
Balthasar	X											
Abram	X											
Sampson	X											
Gregory	X											
Peter									X	X		
Apothecary												
Officer	X											
Lady Montague	X											X
Lady Capulet	X		X		X							X
Juliet			X		X		X			X	X	
Nurse			X		X				X	X		
Citizens	X											X
Guests					X							
Servants		X	X		X							
Others	X			X	X							X
				A	**C**	**T**		**I**				

Figure 3–5. Action Chart for Romeo and Juliet constructed from the playscript for the design process. The chart will be adjusted to reflect casting and doubling once the production has gone into rehearsals.

Romeo & Juliet	III-2	III-3	III-4	III-5	IV-1	IV-2	IV-3	IV-4	IV-5	V-1	V-2	V-3
Chorus												
Escalus-Prince												x
Paris			x		x				x			x
Montague												x
Capulet			x	x		x		x	x			x
Romeo		x		x						x		x
Mercutio												
Benvolio												
Tybalt												
Friar Laurence					x				x		x	x
Friar John											x	
Balthasar										x		x
Abram												
Sampson												
Gregory												
Peter								x				
Apothecary									x			
Officer												
Lady Montague												
Lady Capulet			x	x		x	x	x	x			x
Juliet	x			x	x	x	x					x
Nurse	x	x		x		x	x	x	x			
Citizens												
Guests												
Servants						x		x				
Others									x			x
				A	**C**	**T**		**I**	**I**			

Figure 3–5. *Continued*

scene changes, creating areas and playing spaces, and arranging furniture. You can also use the action chart to gauge one aspect of the play's rhythm: the flow of characters on and off the stage.

VIII. WHAT IS THE PLAY'S THEME?

The core action of *Romeo and Juliet* centers upon the love of the two central characters, their desire to be together, and the hatred and divisions in their world that keep them apart. It seems to be very much a play about divisions that exist in most any society and the essential urge of human hearts—which is larger than any of these divisions—to draw together in love and joy. I

> think, then, that it is important in the story-telling for the love of Romeo and Juliet to be played out against a backdrop of hatred and combat that exists in their world. The first lines of the Prologue introduce this theme, the first scene illustrates it, and the fundamental action of the play is driven by it. (From director's notes, written by Tony Schmitt, in preparation for a production at the Utah Shakespearean Festival)

When you analyze playscripts using all or some of the methods described in this chapter, you will come away knowing a great deal about the play on the page. You will have probed it, poked it, and looked at it from a variety of angles. Now you are ready to expand your perceptions of the script and to grapple with meaning, intention, and creating strong visual statements.

Text Analysis

4

It is a fact of experience that nothing invigorates the imagination more than a spell of sharp thinking.

Eva T. H. Brann, *The World of the Imagination*

Playscript interpretation is not the script itself or the mere passive reflection of it; it is a kind of action. This action is either intrinsic or extrinsic depending upon where it ends up. If one is left with a statement about the work itself, the critic has been intrinsic; if one is left with a statement about history, or the author's life, or the nature of man, or whatnot, the critic has been extrinsic.

Richard Hornby, *Script into Performance*

Once designers have gathered and organized script facts, they can begin to ask questions about meaning, interpretation, and style. Final answers to these questions will, of course, be up to the entire production group; theatrical collaboration is most successful, however, when everyone in the group participates fully in the process. Designers should begin to ask text analysis questions as an integral part of their preparation for the first production meeting. Raising analytical questions and exploring various answers involve a variety of interpretive strategies, some of which are lifted from traditional literary criticism and some from more recent and perhaps more radical literary theories. Others depend on the reader's ability to place the play in its historical context and to understand the various roles theatre has played throughout human history. But perhaps the most important context theatre designers bring to the process of making textual connections is that of current thought, current beliefs, and the contemporary *Zeitgeist*, an essentially untranslatable German word whose overall meaning is considerably richer than its face value translation: spirit of the time.

Text Defined

For clarity in discussing dramatic text analysis, I am defining text in a rather narrow way as: "the sum total of the playwright's intentions and all the intellectual and aesthetic performance potential within the total written work." This definition includes, in part,

1. both the conscious and unconscious intentions of the playwright, including possible influences from the playwright's own life and personal experience
2. the relationship of the play to its own intellectual atmosphere and to subsequent and future streams of thought
3. the resonance of history on the play in its own time, as well as in subsequent and future historical periods
4. the place of the play in the history of theatre, both as script and as performance (as well as the place of certain plays in the history and development of literature)
5. the ways in which the play has been staged and designed, and all potential for staging and designing
6. the reactions of audiences to initial performances of the play, the reactions of subsequent audiences, and the potential for future audience reactions.

It becomes obvious that a play's text extends well beyond the confines of the slender eighty-eight-page playscript I examined at the beginning of chapter 2. It is also obvious that a theatre designer who sets off in the direction of textual analysis is in for a good many side trips along the way. However, in the excitement of poking about in so many byways, it is also important to remember that text analysis must be as firmly grounded in the playwright's words as is the detective work of finding and categorizing clues within the playscript.

Design and Text Analysis

> All human beings by nature stretch themselves out toward knowing. A sign of this is our love of the senses; for even apart from their use, they are loved on their own account, and above all the rest, the one through the eyes. For not only in order that we might act, but even when we are not going to act at all, we prefer seeing, one might say, as against everything else. And the cause is that, among the senses, this one most of all makes us discover things, and makes evident many differences. (Aristotle, *The Metaphysics*, translated by Joe Sachs)

Just how can exploring one or more of the approaches to text analysis help designers locate, house, costume, and illuminate plays? Is text analysis not merely an exercise in academic nit-picking that at best wastes time and at worst actually inhibits creativity? Can there really be any useful relationships between, for example, designing and building a wagon for Mother Courage's business venture in Bertolt Brecht's *Mother Courage and Her Children* and

1. figuring out what the German word *Verfremdung*, usually translated into English as "alienation effect," is all about
2. digging into what Brecht and various literary drama critics have had to say about Epic Theatre
3. trying to make sense of Brecht as playwright, dramatic theorist, and sympathetic Communist, if not Party member
4. exploring the character of Mother Courage
5. learning about the Thirty Years' War
6. looking for connections between the Thirty Years' War and Europe in 1941, the year *Mother Courage* premiered in Zurich
7. asking throughout how contemporary concerns influence the ways in which an audience will respond to a performance of *Mother Courage* today

Finally, even if text analysis can be shown to have a positive effect on the design process, how can a busy designer find the time to become an expert in fields as diverse as dramatic theory and criticism, political science, and European history?

First of all, it is a mistake to approach dramatic text analysis as an academic task, something that resembles a class assignment, or requires consulting a bibliography made up of the dullest sorts of books, or invites consideration of hair-splitting and insignificant details and must result in a formal paper or presentation introduced by some kind of thesis statement.

True text analysis—like a real intellectual workout—is concentrated action. It is the endlessly exciting process of figuring out why a play is put together in its own unique way and of discovering at least a few of the meanings that lurk within it. Text analysis is an intensification of the conversation between the designer and the play that began in the search for facts and structure; only now the conversation includes more voices. Active text analysis illuminates the play and encourages imaging. Ideas, contexts, correlations, and opinions discovered through reading and exploring the broader contexts of the play's world become the basis for choosing the specific images through which an audience will come to know the play.

Second, active text analysis always turns up more questions than answers and should never be pursued in order to prove a point or to substantiate a restricted view of the play, particularly when the designer is still exploring many design possibilities. Recalling that ambiguity is a significant component of plays, the designer must concentrate on discovering diverse, even opposing, points of view whenever he or she is exploring a dramatic text.

Finally, in response to the charge that theatre designers have neither the time nor the expertise to tackle text analysis, I would remind you that you already have more analytical skills than you recognize, and that all creative work requires time and effort if it is to rise above the mundane. There are no simple formulas or quick-and-easy directions for any part of making theatre. Like all art, theatre design comes out of everything the designer is, knows, and experiences, the total content of your knowledge bucket. Every time you begin a project, the first step should be to assess what you already know about the play, the playwright, and the period or periods involved. Then, as time permits, read something you have not read before, look at unfamiliar images, and make new connections; not only will this contribute to the specific project you are working on, it will also add new experiences to your knowledge bucket to use in future designs.

Mother Courage in Context

How might an excursion into text analysis help a designer to ask questions that begin to bring Mother Courage's wagon into focus in his or her imagination and, when the wagon appears in the production, imbue it with visual meaning for the audience?

The following relatively random bits of information were collected by a designer who found them evocative. They come from a variety of sources and demonstrate the kinds of items that contribute to an expanded textual context which can inform the design images for a production of *Mother Courage*.

1. **Verfremdung**

   Neither the play nor the stage production would be required to maintain any consistent illusion of actuality. On the contrary, such illusion was to be destroyed by fragmentation of scenes and settings, by the interruption of action, and by a deliberate severing of suspense. (John Gassner, *Form and Idea in Modern Theatre*)

2. **Epic Theatre** (Brecht's description, 1926)

   To expound the principles of the epic theatre in a few catchphrases is not possible. They still mostly need to be worked out in detail, and include representation by the actor, stage technique, dramaturgy, stage music, use of the film, etc. The essential point of the epic theatre is perhaps that it appeals less to the feelings than to the spectator's reason. Instead of sharing an experience the spectator must come to grips with things. At the same time it would be quite wrong to try and deny emotion to this kind of theatre. (quoted in John Willett's *The Theatre of Bertolt Brecht*)

3. **Brecht and Communism**

   Outwardly, he was for nearly thirty years an orthodox Communist. But he was never a party member, or even a party journalist or speaker. . . . Today, when the Soviet Communist Party has become so widely criticized, not only on intellectual and aesthetic but above all on moral grounds, our judgment of the hard social core of Brecht's work largely depends on what we imagine to be its relation to the official doctrine and official line. (John Willett, *The Theatre of Bertolt Brecht*)

Figure 4–1. *Mother Courage and her wagon, from the production of* Mother Courage and Her Children, *by Bertolt Brecht, at The Shakespeare Theatre, Washington, D.C., with Pat Carroll and Floyd King. Photograph by Joan Marcus.*

Brecht was a very simple person. If you met him in the yard, he might be deep in conversation but he was never so wrapped up that he overlooked one of the workers. He said good morning to a cleaning woman from twenty yards away: the workers soon noted this. (Gerhard R., electrician, quoted in *Brecht as They Knew Him*, edited by Hubert Witt)

4. **The Character of Mother Courage**

Mother Courage is a complex figure. Brecht correctly resisted anyone presenting her primarily as a mother who, "like Niobe," is unable "to protect her children from the vicissitudes of war." For the playwright, Mother Courage is the "merchant-mother," "a great living contradiction who is disfigured and deformed beyond recognition." In the scene on the battlefield she is "truly the hyena." ("Mother Courage and Her Children," by Franz Norbert Mennemeier, in *Brecht: A Collection of Critical Essays*, edited by Peter Demetz)

5. **The Thirty Years' War**

The Thirty Years' War (1618–48) was really four successive wars that began in Bohemia, spread to the rest of the Empire, and finally involved most of the major powers on the Continent. It was a savage and demoralizing conflict that left "Germany poorer and weaker than the western European states. . . . The war sprang out of a complicated mixture of religious and political grievances." (Joseph R. Strayer, Hans W. Gatzke, and E. Harris Harbison, *The Maintream of Civilization Since 1500*)

Then was there naught but beating and burning, plundering, torture, and murder. Most especially was every one of the enemy bent on securing much booty. When a marauding party entered a house, if its master had anything to give he might thereby purchase respite and protection for himself and his family till the next man, who also wanted something, should come along. It was only when everything had been brought forth and there was nothing left to give that the real trouble commenced. (Otto von Guericke, 1631, in *Readings in European History,* edited by James Harvey Robinson)

6. **Mother Courage Premiere, Zurich, April 19, 1941**

Consider what effect the war in progress might have had upon the playwright. Perhaps he read the following report in a newspaper.

Thirty-four people were killed in the cellar ballroom of the Cafe de Paris on March 8, 1941, when a bomb penetrated the ceiling and exploded on the bandstand, wiping out the band and many of the dancers. Nicholas Monsarrat recalls the scene a few moments later:

> The first thing which the rescue squads and the firemen saw . . . was a frieze of other shadowy men, night-creatures who had scuttled within as soon as the echoes ceased, crouching over any . . . corpse they could find . . . ripping off its necklace, or earrings, or brooch. . . .

That vignette suggests the difficulty of piercing the barrier of romantic optimism about human nature implicit in the Allied victory and the resounding Allied extirpation of flagrant evil. . . . One could say of the real war what Barbara Foley has said of the Holocaust—not that it's "unknowable," but "that its full dimensions are inaccessible to the ideological frameworks that we have inherited from the liberal era." (Paul Fussell, *Wartime: Understanding and Behavior in the Second World War*)

7. **A Contemporary Production of *Mother Courage***
   Reflect upon audience awareness and response to the relationship between current events and the events in the play.

   "It is a war. It has started," said Raymond Chretien, who was asked by the United Nations to take a month from his post as Canada's ambassador to the United States, travel to Africa and make recommendations on how the world body should respond to recent conflict involving Zaire, Rwanda and Burundi. . . . Chretien . . . said he fears a repeat of the tribal massacres in Rwanda two years ago. "We would all lose a piece of our soul to accept another genocide of that kind," he said. (*Washington Post*, Thursday, October 31, 1996)

Conversations with a Text

Imagine exploring the wider context of *Mother Courage* with the playscript in one hand and the various notes, books, visual images, journals, and newspapers, to which the journey has taken us, spread out nearby. The designer's challenge is to make connections between everything, script, script facts, and the various contexts in which the play can be considered. What follows are descriptions of two brief designer-play conversations, the kind that might take place in the text analysis process. These interior conversations illustrate how designers use the process, in this case to discover images for Mother Courage's wagon and to consider how an audience might be led to discover something about the meaning of the play by seeing each of those images. Remember that even though these conversations occur inside the designer's head while he or she is thinking, reading, taking notes, drawing, or even engaging in tasks that have nothing whatsoever to do with designing, they begin because the designer sets them in motion. They are intentional, even though they may occur in bits and pieces and the designer cannot always control timing or content.

Subject: Looking for Connections Between Mother Courage and Her Wagon

Mother Courage stays close to her wagon. It is home to her and to her children. It is her transportation from battlefield to battlefield as the war zigzags back and forth across Europe. With the wagon beside her, she can say, *We are in business.* The wagon even contributed to her name.

SERGEANT:	Courage? What kind of name is that?
MOTHER COURAGE:	I was once so scared of going bust I drove my cart right through the bombardment of Riga—right through the heart of it—with fifty loaves of bread in the back. That's why they call me Courage. Mind you, the bread was going mouldy, I didn't have much choice.

When she has a chance to save her second son Swiss Cheese's life by selling the wagon and using the money to bribe the men who have threatened to kill him, she cannot bring herself to do it. *I've only had it seventeen years. I can't. Without money, I'm nothing. Any stranger can kick me in the ditch.* When, in absolute desperation, she finally agrees to the price, knowing she cannot recoup her losses, she is too late to keep him from being shot. *Maybe I haggled too long.* Brecht calls her a "merchant-mother." He puts merchant first. Remember, although Mother Courage is poor and does not have a horse to pull her wagon, she is "in business." Remember also that she loses her first son, Eilif, to the war because she is too busy selling a belt buckle to prevent Eilif from joining up. Brecht connects business and war:

MOTHER COURAGE: To hear them all talk, you'd think these people at the top waged war for the fear of God and in the name of everything that's fine and noble. But just look into it, you'll find they're not that stupid. They're fighting for money. And just as well. Otherwise the little people like you and me wouldn't bother to join in.

and war and order:

SERGEANT: Well, that's the problem, isn't it? They haven't had a war here for such a long time. Without a good war, where do you get your moral standards from? Everything goes to pot in peacetime.

Is Mother Courage proud of her wagon? Does she take excellent care of it? Or, does she take it for granted, much as she does her children? Consider all the things that must come out of it and go into it: belts, shirts, coats, bottles, glasses, plates, shoes, a knife, bullets. . . . All wars seem to be filled with things: things to sell, things to steal and have stolen, things to lose. There must be a great many things in and on the wagon. Perhaps it is even bursting with things, at least until after Swiss Cheese's death. If the audience is to remember that Mother Courage has been "disfigured and deformed beyond recognition" by business and by the war—by war business—she must be in control of enough business for it to be potentially profitable. She is selling, not begging. She expects to make money. Perhaps there are shelves of cups and glasses kept in place by a protective strip of wood. Neat. Orderly. Contemporary designers have to work hard to suggest to their audiences that being in business relates to becoming "disfigured and deformed" because our political and economic systems tell us that being in business is good. Brecht's socialism distrusted business and his Marxism believed that capitalism would destroy itself. What audience members see when they look at the wagon should help them to realize that Mother Courage thinks more of her wagon (her business) than of her children, and to suspect that this attitude will destroy her children and deprive her of everyone she cares for; that she will, in her own businesslike way, perpetuate the war. She takes better care of her wagon than she does of her children. It is well-stocked, tidy, in good repair, clean, jaunty even, at the beginning. Now, what happens to the wagon in the course of the play?

Subject: The Century and/or Decade to Which the Wagon Belongs

> "Neither the play nor the stage production would be required to maintain any consistent illusion of actuality." (Gassner)

> "The essential point of the epic theatre is perhaps that it appeals less to the feelings than to the spectator's reason." (Brecht)

Will the audience think more than they feel if the wagon appears to come from "between 1624 and 1636" and the illusion is that we are in the early seventeenth century? Would a wagon from 1941 (remembering stories of the Okies pulling their broken-down, out-of-gas Ford and Chevy trucks toward California) be more apt to make them think about the issues raised by the play? Could the wagon have any sort of relationship with the 1990s? Is it perhaps some visual combination of the three? What about: A metal frame and tongue, wagon bed and upright structure of wood, fabric curtains or cover, rubber truck tires?

Remember: before you can start a thought conversation with a text, you must first put things into your head to think about: facts from the playscript, everything you can recall from your own memory that might relate to the play, and a selection of new information and experiences. Be patient. Don't push too hard and don't expect to come up with neat answers in a short time. Neat answers may well appear (several of them usually do), but it takes time for them to crystallize.

Text Analysis and Theatre Education

> Wonderful brilliance may be gained for human judgment by getting to know men. We are all huddled and concentrated in ourselves, and our vision is reduced to the length of our nose. Socrates was asked where he was from. He replied not "Athens," but "The world." He, whose imagination was fuller and most extensive, embraced the universe as his city, and distributed his knowledge, his company, and his affections to all mankind, unlike us who look only at what is underfoot. (Michel de Montaigne, "On the Education of Children, 1579–80")

Come to the theatre. Did you see the last moments of Terence Rattigan's *Separate Tables*? The residents of a *pension* sit in frigid isolation under the harsh

> lights of their dining room. Events bring them to feel some sympathy for each other, and the angel of compassion enters the room. The harsh light dims. The tiny table lamps, unnoticed in the brightness, now cast their warm pools. The room, the characters, and the play are charmed as the curtain falls.
>
> A good idea. Whose idea? The author's? The director's? Even—God forbid—the actors? Why not? Must ideas like this be the sole property of someone who knows how to calculate voltage drop in a series circuit? (David Hays, *Light on the Subject*)

Until well into the twentieth century, the relatively small percentage of people in the United States who received higher or postsecondary education studied virtually the same subjects, read the same authors, and discussed similar ideas, both historical and contemporary. No educated person in the early years of this century could have overlooked Darwin's theory of natural selection, Freud's exploration of the unconscious, or Marx and Engels's predictions of economic revolution. It would not have occurred to an educated person at that time to explain why he or she was not familiar with major social and intellectual issues of the day by saying: "But I'm an art major. I never took courses in biology or political science." Three-quarters of a century later, with more than half of all Americans earning degrees past high school, educated people no longer share a common intellectual background, have not read the same books, and are much less aware of ideas and discoveries in fields other than their own than educated people were seventy-five years ago. Most college students in the United States concentrate their undergraduate studies in specialized areas, such as accounting, environmental science, historic preservation, computer science, studio art, and so on. The subjects that once constituted the bulk of the undergraduate curriculum have been reduced to a dozen or so required courses that are referred to as the general education, or core, curriculum. Even in those liberal arts institutions that retain a strong commitment to a curriculum with a healthy dose of literature, critical thinking, art, math, and science, most students expend far more mental energy on their area of specialization than on the "gen-ed" requirements. It is all too common for Americans with undergraduate and graduate degrees from excellent colleges and universities to be completely unaware of ideas and theories from other fields. Even within individual disciplines, specialization has become so intense that someone who has concentrated on a subspecialty may have no idea of what is going on in other areas of the same field.

The changes in theatre education in American colleges and universities from the 1960s to the present mirror what has occurred in the academy at large. Theatre classes were first offered in American institutions of higher learning in the 1920s and achieved academic legitimacy by being taught under the auspices of English departments. The emphasis was on dramatic literature and in some places playwrighting. Play production remained precisely what it had been since the flowering of universities in the Middle Ages: an extracurricular activity. Over the next two decades, however, autonomous theatre departments gradually emerged on the higher education scene and produced plays under their own sponsorship and guidance. With only a few exceptions, however, the focus of theatre studies in most of these institutions was academic, rather than on the performance or professional aspects of theatre.

A revolution in theatre education began in the 1960s, hand in hand with the other social and political revolutions associated with that explosive decade. The emphasis of many theatre programs changed from teaching a wide cross section of students *about* theatre to training a highly motivated group of students to *do* theatre. Undergraduate and graduate theatre departments sprang up all over the country, often aligning themselves with studio art and music performance programs (which were undergoing a similar professionalization). Some theatre departments began to call themselves professional theatre training programs. The master of fine arts, or MFA, degree was born and became recognized as a "terminal" degree for college and university teachers who taught in the fine and performing arts. Enrolling in MFA programs has taken the place of apprenticeships and conservatory training for young professional artists. Only a limited number of universities had ever offered the Ph.D. in any branch of theatre studies, and some of these programs were abandoned in favor of the MFA. At universities where Ph.D. programs in theatre continued to operate, academics and professionals tended to settle down on opposite sides of the philosophical—and pedagogical—fence, each group looking down its collective nose at the other.

On the undergraduate level, two approaches to theatre education were devised. Although the actual requirements of both approaches vary a good deal from institution to institution, they remain the primary options for students who wish to major in theatre. Students can attend a school offering a theatre major within a broad-based bachelor of arts program (BA), or enroll in a college or university where they can earn a bachelor of fine arts degree (BFA). In BA programs the number of theatre courses theatre majors can take is limited, usually less than a quarter of the total number required for graduation, and they are expected to explore other disciplines as well as to complete a fairly hefty number of general education requirements, which usually include classes in literature, history, mathematics, science, philosophy, and a foreign language. In BFA programs, students become theatre specialists, taking half or even more of their classes in theatre subjects. The general education requirements are less rigorous than those for the BA, and often do not include mathematics, philosophy, or a foreign language.

Along with these changes in theatre education, a professional theatre revolution was also in progress. Throughout the 1960s and 1970s, theatre decentralized away from New York City and Broadway, and into dozens of large and middle-sized cities from coast to coast. The regional theatre movement of these decades altered the professional lives of thousands of young actors, directors, playwrights, and designers. No longer did they troop like lemmings to New York or Los Angeles to seek their fortunes; instead, they found challenging, gainful employment in Minneapolis, Houston, Atlanta, Denver, Seattle, Providence, New Haven, and Hartford. The establishment of the National Endowment for the Arts in 1964 brightened the financial and spiritual future for professional, nonprofit theatres, and over the next twenty years the number of companies increased from half a dozen to more than two hundred. As regional theatres attracted larger and larger audiences, the quality of physical productions soared, and by the mid-1970s there were jobs for more and more well-trained theatre artisans and technicians as well as for actors, directors, and designers. Many theatre departments responded by increasing curriculum specialization on the graduate and undergraduate levels.

Today, undergraduate theatre students can choose to concentrate on performance, design, or technology, even in some BA programs, while BFA programs have devised curricula that allow intensive specialization. Among the most extreme, for example, are institutions at which an eighteen-year-old theatre major can embark on a four-year professional theatre training program in costume technology that will include fewer than a dozen courses in any subject other than those directly related to building costumes and costume properties. In other words, a student can earn a BFA degree in theatre, with a specialty in costume technology, without ever performing in or directing a play, stage managing, designing a set, or focusing a light. And it goes almost without saying that literature and history in general, and theatre literature, criticism, and history in particular, have a very small place, or no place, in many undergraduate professional theatre training curricula. In some BFA programs, theatre history is taught only in relationship to the plays that are produced each term; if Molière does not turn up on the production calendar during your four years, you could easily graduate without knowing anything about Molière's plays, his theatre, or his place in the theatre continuum. Not only are theatre students, like most students today, strangers to ideas from the traditional disciplines like philosophy and history, as well as newer fields like neurobiology and computer science, they are equally unaware of the important role theatre has played in human history and cannot discuss even the most recent events taking place in the American theatre.

Students with specialized theatre educations become specialized theatre professionals with admirable artistic and technical skills. Specialization is most intense in curricula created to train theatre technicians, but it is also intense in theatre design programs. Designers learn to draw and paint beautifully and to understand and manipulate the elements of design and the principles of composition. Costume designers explore and manipulate the effects of clothing on the human body; scenic designers alter the geometry of the stage space; lighting designers work subtle magic on audience emotions. Many of them, however, do their work in a peculiar sort of isolation from the play and from the theatrical event. Yes, they are intensely concerned with their own work and the development of their own individual skills, and yes, they are serious and hard-working, but in general, they have little or no passion for the theatre at large or even, in many cases, the theatrical event for which they do their individual jobs to perfection. They are only vaguely aware of what is happening in theatres across the country—a new play in Chicago, a designer in Boston who has given a new look to an old opera, a theatre in San Francisco producing contemporary Japanese plays. They know nothing at all about recent theatre history in their own country, and only the most basic facts about general theatre history in the West. Worst of all, very few of these designers have any sense of theatre as a cultural force or as a response to basic human instincts. Too many American theatre designers are working harder than ever to make technically proficient theatre, but to no particular purpose.

Yet the most basic purpose of all theatrical events is to create intellectual, social, political, and emotional connections between theatre and people. The specific nature of these connections is unique to live theatre, and no other art or entertainment can match its immediacy or intensity. Theatre designers who make their own individual connections with the plays they design have an important rolc to play in invoking and realizing the power of performances to connect deeply with audiences. The text analysis in which they engage is intense, bold, creative, far-reaching, and closely reasoned. Designers who approach texts in these ways learn and grow with every design. They look for and find whatever they need to know, when they need to know it. Text analysis may at first be more difficult for those designers with a more specialized than liberal education, but then, nobody who works in the theatre expects the job to be easy.

I end this section with three comments from a discussion about the lack of background, mostly literary, in the work of young theatre designers. (All are from "A Roof Without a House," *Theatre Crafts*, March 1985.)

> Unless stiff requirements steer students in the right direction, only an ambitious minority will select a semester of the seventeenth-century literature, nineteenth-century European history, early twentieth-century psychology, and Renaissance music. But those are precisely the resources a future stage designer will need when handed *La Boheme* or *The Revenger's Tragedy.* (Susan Lieberman)

> When Ali Nagler spoke at Yale about *Don Giovanni* last year, the students didn't seem very responsive; they didn't ask questions. So I asked, "Okay, how many of you know *Don Giovanni?*" And not one of them did. Then I asked, "How many of you know Molière's *Don Juan?*" And not one of them did. Then I asked, "How many of you know *Man and Superman?*" About half of them had read it. Finally I asked, "How could you read *Don Juan in Hell* without associating it with *Don Juan* or *Don Giovanni?*" Well, they hadn't really thought about it. (Ming Cho Lee)

> We have created a Russian Easter egg—very beautiful on the outside, but no content inside. A drawing might be gorgeous, but will it help the actor? Does it express the play? Because of the way young designers are taught, they have no resources to deal with anything other than the crust of things. (John Jensen)

Literary Theory

5

[W]hat I have tried to show throughout this book is that the history of modern literary theory is part of the political and ideological history of our epoch. From Percy Bysshe Shelley to Norman N. Holland, literary theory has been indissociably bound up with political beliefs and ideological values. Indeed literary theory is less an object of intellectual enquiry in its own right than a particular perspective in which to view the history of our times. Nor should this be in the least cause for surprise. For any body of theory concerned with human meaning, value, language, feeling and experience will inevitably engage with broader, deeper beliefs about the nature of human individuals and societies, problems of power and sexuality, interpretations of past history, versions of the present and hopes for the future.

Terry Eagleton, *Literary Theory*

Poetry is an effort to find out what one really thinks.

Richard Hugo

It was also the time [1934] when interpretation and production were being influenced by modern realism, with the effect that human truth had come to be considered more important than the famous "music of words" the result was that rhetoric or lyrical delirium had to go. It was then that I understood, more clearly than I have ever done with Racine and Corneille, how poetry is better able to express reality than the so-called "realistic" language of everyday life; and how style is the only penetrating instrument of authentic "realism," whatever the period.

Michel Saint-Denis, *Theatre: The Rediscovery of Style*

> The important critic is the person who is absorbed in the present problems of art, and who wishes to bring the forces of the past to bear upon the solution of these problems.
>
> T. S. Eliot, *The Sacred Wood*

> Let us here deal with Poetry, its essence and its several species, with the characteristic function of each species and the way in which plots must be constructed if the poem is to be a success; and also with the number and character of the constituent parts of a poem, and similarly with all other matters proper to this same inquiry; and let us, as nature directs, begin first with first principles.
>
> Aristotle, *Poetics*

What do literary studies have to do with theatre design? Nothing and a lot. I do not even attempt to argue with the fact that a theatre designer can work successfully for a lifetime without ever turning to the professional output of literary critics and theorists for help or inspiration. Theatre designers work at drawing boards, in shops, and on stages; they create tangible objects and evocative atmospheres for live theatrical performances. Literary critics and theorists (a professional group that includes specialists in dramatic criticism and theory) are primarily thinkers and observers. They read, study, categorize, interpret, and reinterpret the literary output of writers past and present and the work of other literary critics past and present. How do these two seemingly very different professional activities effect each other? Is there, for example, a relationship between the work of a scholar who conceives of, researches, and writes an essay examining the impact of Beaumarchais' *The Marriage of Figaro* on French revolutionary groups in the late eighteenth century, and the creative process of a late twentieth-century designer creating the theatrical environment for a production of Bertolt Brecht's *Mother Courage*? Can these professional activities cross paths at any point? I believe they can, and that many designs will be substantially enriched by the interaction.

The discoveries of a theatre designer in any area of contextual analysis never constitute the entire visual input for a production. Their effect on the design process is more like that of a pungent spice on a savory stew. By itself, the spice has a unique definition and is rich in potential, but it does not constitute a meal. In combination with meat, vegetables, broth, and other seasonings, however, it can turn a commonplace dish into a memorable eating experience, even if the diners enjoying the meal are unaware of its presence. The blending of elements in cooking is an excellent metaphor for the way in which theatre designers blend basic script information and selected spicy ideas into rich, evocative designs.

Literary Criticism and Literary Theory

> Disagreements about literature do not imply that the task of criticism is futile, or that majority opinion rules, or that all opinions are equally good. Whether the critic is engaged in analysis, interpretation, or evaluation, discussion is valuable in many ways as a stimulus and aid to understanding. The responsibility of the critic is to make the experience of literature fuller and richer, more informed intellectually and emotionally. (M. M. Liberman and Edward E. Foster, *A Modern Lexicon of Literary Terms*)

Literary criticism and literary theory are somewhat different and a lot alike. *Criticism*, from the Greek word *kritikos*, means "one who discerns, judges, and discusses." At its best, criticism is informed discussion about a particular literary work or group of works. Literary theory takes a step away from individual works, concerned instead with the place and nature of literature in art and in society.

Aristotle's *Poetics* is a work of literary theory. In it, Aristotle examines the human need for imitative activities and points out how this need is met through various sorts of imitative or theatrical events to which he gives the generic name poetry. The focus of the work is a careful study of the nature of poetry carried out by way of personal observations. Aristotle identifies the elements common to imitative works and discusses the compositional strategies behind theatrical events that educate and improve individuals and human society. Because Aristotle's *Poetics* has survived, and remains a sturdy foundation for all subsequent literature studies, literary theory can claim to be an older form of study than literary criticism.

Traditionally, as Liberman and Foster comment, literary criticism has been primarily concerned with the analysis, interpretation, and evaluation of literary works. Nowadays we single out many specialized forms of literary criticism, including, for example, biographical criticism and historical criticism, in which the background and experiences of the author or the place of the work in its historical context is the focus of the investigation.

There are at least a dozen different definitions of literature and at least twice that many approaches to the study of literature. Some scholars distinguish literature from nonliterature simply by way of its "invented quality." Others insist that literature should be defined according to some predetermined value scale. Still others insist that a literary work be identified by its capacity for stimulating the moral imagination. Within the professional world of literary criticism and literary theory, various points of view are maintained in a lively and often somewhat adversarial atmosphere. The proponents of each approach insist that their ideas are the most revealing and will result in a deeper understanding of the work or works being studied.

Fortunately, a working theatre designer is free to ignore professional literary debates about which critical theory is best. Indeed, I would advise designers to avoid taking sides in all disagreements between critics and theorists and simply put the ideas that are most appropriate to their individual interests and the needs of the play to use. Designers who wish to add active dramatic text analysis to their battery of design skills should acquire a basic understanding of classical and modern critical theories and keep up, even if only in a general way, with current critical ideas. A specific project may require in-depth reading about particular ideas or in the work of specific writers. But not every design project will be enriched by critical writings that interpret the work itself or examine the period, genre, or any other classification into which it falls. New plays, for instance, generally have no critical environment until they have been given several productions. A great many plays are thought to be too insignificant for critical consideration, although contemporary criticism, with its strong interest in popular culture, has almost specialized in reinterpreting older works that were neglected by the critics of their day. Recent critical studies carried out with a specific gender, racial, or political emphasis provide particularly interesting, and visually evocative ideas. Many designers would not tackle a production of Shakespeare's *The Taming of a Shrew* anytime in the near future, for example, without at least dipping into the work of feminist critical theorists such as Sue-Ellen Case and Julia Kristeva.

It is important to reemphasize my point that nothing a theatre designer discovers in any piece of literary criticism or theory will constitute the sole basis for any theatrical design. The design process is a collaboration between one designer's various trains of thought as much as it is a collaboration between the members of the production team. The mental image I described in chapter 1 of human knowledge as a bucket of water into which new experiences are constantly dropping, rearranging what is already known, is a useful way of thinking about how the design process works. Each time a designer begins to concentrate on a specific piece of work, the totality of what he or she brings to the process at that particular time will be unique to that project. During the process, an idea from a critic or a theorist can be just the catalyst needed to ignite the designer's sensibilities and throw a wholly new light on the play's physical environment.

Ideas in the Air

Even without being consciously aware of it, theatre designers read plays with attitudes heavily influenced not only by literary critics and theorists but also by other thinkers and writers whose thoughts and writings have shaped the way society sees itself. The extent to which theatre design reflects the ideas that define society at any given time never ceases to amaze me. Who first perceives the ideas and how they spread throughout the theatrical community are as much a mystery as the identity of the wag who told the original knock-knock joke and how it spread into a knock-knock epidemic.

Equally mysterious is the cause-and-effect relationship between the theatre of any period and that period's beliefs about human nature and human organization, that is, about society and politics. We can easily accept the fact that theatre reflects the spirit of its time, and there are many indisputable indications that the spirit of every historical period has been, and continues to be, affected by the nature of its theatrical events. This relationship is a classic chicken versus egg situation; it is impossible to determine which begets which. The same is, of course, true of novels, poetry, films, painting, architecture, and so on. Each art form is influenced by what a culture believes about human nature and human society, and, conversely, all cultural beliefs are influenced by their intellectual and artistic icons.

Did you ever stop to wonder where the "eclectic" (a word that means, in part, "composed of elements drawn from various sources") approach to theatre design originated? Who was the first designer (director? playwright?) to come up with the idea of deliberately mixing periods and styles in the same production? Who first imagined it would be successful? And how did the idea spread so fast?

Although it is impossible to plot the precise rise and flow of this particular design theory from designer to designer, or from theatre to theatre, it is obvious that eclectic design is the visual response to a literary theory known as deconstructionism. This is true even though many designers who use these ideas to inform their visual images know nothing at all about the theory or about Jacques Derrida, the French philosopher and linguist who is generally considered to be the father of deconstructionism. Deconstructionism is a big set of ideas that has successfully made its escape from the confines of scholarly books and journals and is out in the air for everyone to sniff.

It was more than a decade after deconstructionism had become an acceptable topic for discussion among literary theorists that it began to make an impact on American theatre design. Prior to the 1980s, few American theatre companies would have dared to mount a production of *Macbeth* with costumes, props, and settings suggesting five different centuries. By 1990, eclectic designs were commonplace.

The literary theorist Terry Eagleton describes deconstructionism in his 1983 book, *Literary Theory.* As you read his description, see if you can relate it to any examples of eclectic design (which some people call postmodernist, a much more general and inclusive term, and a bit harder to define) you have seen in the last half-dozen years.

> [The works of some deconstructionists] cast grave doubt upon the classical notions of truth, reality, meaning and knowledge, all of which could be exposed as resting on a naively representational theory of language. If meaning, the signified, was a passing product of words or signifiers, always shifting and unstable, part-present and part-absent, how could there be any determinate truth or meaning at all? If reality was constructed by our discourse rather than reflected by it, how could we ever know reality itself, rather than merely knowing our own discourse? Was all talk just talk about our talk? Did it make sense to claim that one interpretation of reality, history or the literary text was "better" than another?

This interesting notion—vastly simplified!—is that what is meant, or signified, by a word or a group of words changes: through time, from one encounter to another, and according to context. The theory also raises the intriguing question: does language reflect real experiences, or is language a means of creating reality through discourse? I am because I say I am! Once we grow mildly obsessed with thinking about language cut loose from its simple narrative and representational moorings, we are ready to begin to read playscripts through a variety of lenses and from several different angles. We accept the fact that we are not combing through a text for the right answer, or even for a best or most truthful version. We begin to see the language of plays as a vehicle for exploring uncharted wildernesses that defy mapping and must be rediscovered in each decade as the dynamics of human institutions and society change.

Shakespeare's *Henry V* was written in 1599 and the events of the play reflect actual historical events, including a particularly famous and much studied battle, Agincourt, which was fought on October 25, 1415. A designer working on a production of *Henry V* usually begins the work with research into the real events upon which Shakespeare based his play. At some point in the process, however, the designer cannot help but make connections with the text that include universal references to characteristics of soldiers and soldiering and specific references to battles that occurred long after Agincourt and in every century up to the present.

Few battles occur in any age that do not begin with exhortations from leaders to men about bravery and soldierly behavior. The following lines from King Henry's famous speech to his men in the midst of the siege at Harfleur even conjure up the twentieth-century basic-training exercises intended to turn young men into warriors:

> In peace there's nothing so becomes a man
> As modest stillness and humility;
> But when the blast of war blows in our ears,
> Then imitate the action of the tiger:
> Stiffen the sinews, conjure up the blood,
> Disguise fair nature with hard-favored rage;
> Then lend the eye a terrible aspect:
> Let it pry through the portage of the head
> Like the brass cannon; let the brow o'erwhelm it
> As fearfully as doth a gallèd rock,
> O'erhang and jutty his confounded base,

Swilled with the wild and wasteful ocean.
Now set the teeth, and stretch the nostril wide,
Hold hard the breath, and bend up every spirit
To his full height!

Henry V, act 3, scene 1

Much later in the play, King Henry speaks to his officers and men, who by this time are tired, sick, and greatly outnumbered. He predicts the future behavior of those who will survive the battle, behavior many Americans have seen in their own families. When one designer reads this speech, for example, he remembers a great-uncle who was with the U.S. 4th Division that landed on Utah Beach in Normandy on Tuesday, June 6, 1944, in the World War II military operation known as D day, and who never tired of recounting his experiences on that momentous occasion. "I never read those words without thinking Shakespeare is talking about my Uncle Ed."

He that outlives this day, and comes safe home,
Will stand a-tiptoe when this day is named,
And rouse him at the name of Crispian.
He that shall see this day, and live old age,
Will yearly on the vigil feast his neighbors
And say, "Tomorrow is Saint Crispian."
Then will he strip his sleeve and show his scars,
And say, "These wounds I had on Crispin's day."
Old men forget; yet all shall be forgot,
But he'll remember, with advantages,
What feats he did that day.

Henry V, act 4, scene 3

Having breathed the air of deconstructionism, it does not require a giant imaginative leap for a designer to begin to visualize a battlefield that reflects, in part, World War I trenches, a wheat field trampled by Pickett's charge, and a muddy track in the Vietnam jungle. Pouches, bags, boots, belts, hats, and clothing items might suggest these and other battles. The effect may be subtle, with, for example, every soldier, no matter how dressed, using weapons from the fifteenth century. In a more overt visual statement, the weapons

(a)

Figure 5–1. Here are three photographs from a 1995 production of Henry V at The Shakespeare Theatre in Washington, D.C., which combine contemporary and period elements in the costumes. I find the ordinary striped shirt worn by the Boy particularly evocative of the fate of children in all wars. (a) Derek Smith as Prince Hal in stage armor and chain mail. Photograph by Carol Pratt. (b) Antonio Pearly McQueen IV as the Boy. Photograph by Carol Rosegg. (c) David Sabin as Gower and Jarlath Conroy as Fluellen. Notice the contemporary shirts under stage armor that has a period look. Photograph by Carol Rosegg.

(b)

(c)

Figure 5–1. *Continued*

themselves might range from longbows to automatic machine guns. The first time an audience experiences an eclectic design, it may be confused or even shocked. But audience members are breathing deconstructed air also and it will not be long before they begin to make the appropriate connections. From a contemporary perspective, the language of war is indeed a shifting reality.

Another group of ideas we absorb as we live and breathe the *Zeitgeist* of our particular time and place in history has to do with the power and influence of popular culture. Since the middle of the twentieth century, many branches of scholarship have concerned themselves specifically with the lives and experiences of ordinary people, particularly those groups that have usually been left out by the older, more traditional scholarly disciplines. This movement is well represented in American colleges and universities, where African American, Latin American, Asian, Gay and Lesbian, and Women's Studies programs have become well established. Following the same bent, both art historians and literary scholars have increasingly turned their attention to popular art and literature. It is not unusual to find high schools and colleges offering courses on cartoon art, jazz, or genre writing such as science fiction or mysteries. Popular culture itself is now a legitimate field of study in which students may earn undergraduate and graduate degrees.

Most scholars agree that the literature of every culture, which includes oral narrative and many kinds of performance as well as a body of writing, reflects that culture's most fundamental beliefs about human nature and the nature and traditions of its own civilization. Literature also serves as one of society's most potent weapons for preserving or attacking those beliefs. It follows quite naturally that political theories and literary theories have deep, interconnecting roots.

Theatre, more than any other art form, has the power to connect the immediate present with any and every other moment in human history and to challenge us all to examine past events from a contemporary perspective. A theatrical event happens at a given time and place. It is always a present-moment interaction between performers and audience members. Both groups carry their knowledge buckets to the theatre, and everybody leaves with more than they came in with, including an increased potential for making connections. The richer the theatrical event, the deeper and more evocative the connections.

The Shifting Present

A scene designer who has encountered Caryl Churchill's *Cloud Nine* on three separate occasions, recalls with some surprise how much his own personal relationship with the script changed from one time to the next, and how much each response reflected "what was in the air" when he was doing his work.

> The script was pretty new the first time I designed it and the cross-dressing in the first act was a good deal more shocking than it was ten years later. Gender was the big issue, although I don't think we used the word gender all that much in those days. We were certainly focused on what was male and what was female. I remember sketching jungle foliage which was blatantly suggestive of male and female sex organs. We had those leaves and stalks waving all around that proper British establishment, while those damned Victorians tried to mask their sexuality under swags and fringes and meticulously manicured potted plants. That production was all about sex, but so were we, and so was everything out there in the world.
>
> The next production was a bit more than ten years later. Sex had been done to death. Cross-dressing was old hat and gender definitions were on the back burner. But homosexual rights, or the lack of same, were making headlines. I don't think we actually talked about making homosexuality the big theme and I doubt if it was anybody's conscious intention to do that. But we did. Rather than contrasting maleness and femaleness, we made a world where it was just as normal, maybe even more normal, to love somebody of your own sex as somebody of the opposite sex. In our meetings we talked more about the second act than about the first act. Visually, the two acts became a blending thing.
>
> In 1994 I reread *Cloud Nine* and was obsessed by the theme of power. I remember thinking: This play is about power structures. It's about politics, colonialism, racial superiority, gender superiority, and the tyranny of family. There's even a bit of child abuse. All the other stuff was still there but this time I saw it through what I was reading about in newspapers and seeing on talk shows and on TV news: power struggles on every level. It was a different play; the same play, but a different play. I'm ready to design it again. A new, updated version.

Connections Between Then and Now

The relationship between a society and its art forms, including theatre, would be far less problematic—but also far less interesting to theatre designers and literary theorists—if it was static rather than dynamic. If, for example, someone had hit upon a satisfactory, time-tested, cause-and-effect description of the human condition that could serve indefinitely, each generation would be spared the angst of trying yet again to understand the meaning of life, of disagreeing with all previous answers, of redefining everything and then changing its own mind at regular intervals. Humanity, by its very nature, is doomed to the fate of incessantly looking at things in new ways.

Human thoughts have never been quiescent, not even in the slow-moving Middle Ages. People whose lives span some, or most, of the twentieth century have experienced continual and significant shifts in the ways we understand ourselves and interact on the most basic levels with the world in which we live. Indeed, the changes occur so continually that we do not even see how much our lives and our perceptions of the world around us have changed unless we make a deliberate effort to do so. Inventive writing documents these changes. Some writing does this consciously through the work of authors who reach back in time to recapture past events. Other works emerge directly from their own time and invite us in to live for a little while in another age. Dramatic writing, from the Greeks on, gives us the hands-down best opportunities to experience who and where we have been and to make dynamic connections with our present circumstances.

As society changes, words record, perpetuate, and legitimize what is occurring. For the succeeding generation, for whom the new social order is no longer new but simply accepted as the way things are, language stabilizes and defines the status quo. Every hiccough in society prompts subtle alterations in language. Social upheavals such as those the United States experienced in the 1860s, the 1930s, and the 1960s are accompanied by significant changes in what people say and mean, as well as by the appearance of new words and phrases. Scientific and technological developments produce a fountain of new words as well as streams of new uses for old words.

Every idea that is thought, written, and released into the intellectual atmosphere eventually turns up somewhere in literature. Literature tells us who we are; literature also tells us who we were. Literature may even be part of the process by which we invent ourselves. All the literary and word-based arts connect human thoughts and actions with social institutions and national character. None produces as dynamic an experience as the theatrical event.

Images of Poetry

The theatre designer Robert Edmund Jones ends a chapter called "Light and Shadow in the Theatre," in his book, *The Dramatic Imagination*, with these words:

> The creative approach to the problem of stage lighting—the art, in other words, of knowing where to put light on the stage and where to take it away—is not a matter of textbooks or precepts. There are no arbitrary rules. There is only a goal and a promise. We have the mechanism with which to create this ideal, exalted, dramatic light in the theatre. Whether we can do so or not is a matter of temperament as well as of technique. The secret lies in our perception of light in the theatre as something alive.
>
> Does this mean that we are to carry images of poetry and vision and high passion in our minds while we are shouting out orders to electricians on ladders in light-rehearsals?
>
> Yes. This is what it means.

In today's professional world of intense specialization, I am deeply concerned that theatre designers acquire the sensibilities and skills that will allow them "to carry images of poetry and vision and high passion" in their minds while they work at their increasingly complex, and highly demanding, technical tasks. When in their training or experience do today's theatre designers develop deep connections with literature in general and dramatic literature in particular? Where and when do they become conversant with the critical and philosophical ideas that constitute the poetic, visionary, and passionate foundation of our theatre? How can they imagine, much less carry, a vision of "a brilliant fresh theatre" when they have little or no sense of how contemporary theatre came to be? Obviously, the most direct route to sharpening one's sense of poetry is to read as much as possible, as widely as possible, and as deeply as possible. (Nowadays, with so much good writing, including fiction, poetry, and drama, available on audiotapes, listening is also a way of making connections with literature.) I hope I have made the case for opening one's head to a host of ideas by becoming acquainted with the work of literary critics and theorists past and present. Read their books and essays for interest and for information and resist getting hung up on jargon.

At a time when more and more people have been led to believe that they are incapable of doing a job if they have not been trained in a formal program that legitimizes their acquisition of all necessary skills with a license and/or an appropriate acronym, many of us assume we cannot learn what we have not been taught. This, of course, is nonsense. We do not need degrees in literary studies to become worthy readers. We do not need courses in literary theory in order to read and understand works by literary theorists. We can apply the ideas we find in dramatic texts and literary studies without being assigned to do so by a teacher.

The book list for chapter 5, located in the back of this book, includes a few specific titles I have found useful, and serves as a brief introduction to the types of books that can contribute to text analysis for theatre designers.

Theatre Yesterday and Today

6

Of what is called the drama, or dramatic presentation in the United States, as now put forth at the theatre, I should say it deserves to be treated with the same gravity, and on a par with the questions of ornamental confectionery at public dinners, or the arrangement of curtains and hangings in a ball-room—nor more, nor less.

Walt Whitman, *Democratic Vistas*, 1874

The state, like everything else, has itself to support. It rests with itself to decide whether a noble and non-commercial theatre is more beneficial to its health than a degraded and money-making theatre; and the difficult task it sets itself is to discern the difference between a noble theatre and a claptrap theatre. The latter class of theatre can be observed any day from the comfortable seat of a hansom cab if the driver is directed to go down Shaftesbury Avenue, the Haymarket, then down to St. James' Palace, back through Pall Mall into St. Martin's Lane and then down the Strand. The non-commercial theatre must be imagined . . . and when once it has been imagined by the artist the State has the power to assist in the realization of the dream.

Edward Gordon Craig, *A Production*, 1930

[M]ost of the significant work in the American theatre during the 1980's took place in not-for-profit organizations. . . . Outside of New York, there were more than 200 not-for-profit theatres, which together mounted about 2,500 productions a year. They varied considerably in size, facilities, total program, and quality, but they offered live performances in almost all parts of the United States. Several played a major role in American theatrical life.

Oscar G. Brockett and Robert Findlay, *Century of Innovation*, 1991

Theatre designers, as a group, are not often the agents of change and upheaval in the course of theatre history. Only a handful of designers have ever seriously disturbed the theatrical status quo by starting their own alternative theatres, writing nonmainstream plays, or creating controversial productions. Once we have completed our education and training, most of us—from the ancient Greek designers who carved wooden masks by hand to present day lighting designers whose work is supported by a vast electronic technology—are relatively content to work in the theatre of our own day. Designers may gripe about their theatre, about working conditions, fees, budgets, the kind and quality of the playscripts and performances their work supports, but in general they accept the status quo and consciously and unconsciously shape their work to meet current demands.

Problems arise when the character and conditions of theatre production change and a designer awakes one morning to find that the theatre in which he or she has been working is moving off in a different direction from yesterday. Such changes, of course, never happen overnight, but from the perceptions of a typically busy, continually preoccupied designer, it seems so. Quite suddenly, the relationship of this designer with each part of the design process undergoes subtle alterations. A different type of script is being produced (shorter, perhaps, with fewer characters, more locations, and disjointed dialogue); a dramaturg is part of the production group; the director presses for designs that express a "postmodernist sensibility"; the production is being shared between several theatres, making it necessary for the sets and lighting to work in very different spaces; the building period is shorter, and the budget smaller.

Let us suppose that this designer is one of many whose professional career began in the late 1970s, when the Regional Theatre Movement in the United States was at its height. The National Endowment for the Arts had been established in 1964 and was providing increasing prominence, along with minimal but significant funding, for what some were calling our new, national theatre: the nearly two hundred regional professional theatres that had sprung up all across the country in a mere twenty years. Our typical designer may live in Denver but work in a half-dozen different cities and towns in as many states. Over the past twelve to fifteen years, this designer's work has provided one or more of the visual components for a standard repertory of plays, including works by Shakespeare, Molière, Anton Chekhov, George Bernard Shaw, Eugene O'Neill, Arthur Miller, and Tennessee Williams, and for a smattering of new plays. During this time the theatre organizations themselves have expanded, built new and additional performance spaces, and increased their outreach activities in their various communities. Individually and collectively, these theatres seem to this designer to be what theatre is and what it was meant to be. The future appears certain to hold more of the same: greater stability, larger audiences, a new computerized light board, additional personnel in the scene and costume shops, and always, bigger budgets.

Yet the single certainty that exists in the continually shifting cycles of theatre history (and by natural extension human history) is the certainty of constant change. Every shift in events—intellectual, social, political, military, or most especially, economic—reverberates in the performing arts, while great shifts, those booming events that invariably seem to come from out of the blue, often turn the theatrical status quo on its ear.

At the end of the twentieth century, our typical theatre designer, wondering where the old, established theatre has gone and trying to figure out what the new organization will demand, may decide to step back from the intense day-to-day involvement in which most designers lose themselves and attempt to put present events into a broader context. Questions arise. What was American theatre like before the NEA? Before there was a Guthrie Theatre? A Denver Theatre Center? Before there were Shakespeare theatres in a dozen states? Where did theatre designers work? What kind of work did they do? Maybe, just maybe, this designer can get some bearing on where theatre is going by finding out where it has been.

There can be no doubt whatsoever in the mind of any seriously committed theatre designer that the process of designing every play is closely related to the kind of theatre for which the work is being done. The way individual theatre organizations operate at any given time is interconnected with how theatre is being described and defined as a whole by society at large. Understanding the nature of one's own contemporary theatre, and being able to sense it as a living, changing institution, is yet another context in which designers read and analyze the plays they design.

Business or Art?

> The current confusion in politics is in trying to define capitalism as an ethical system. The arts are a repository for ideas: ethics, ideology, ideals. But if you reduce the arts to an economic system, what happens to traditions? (Daryl Chin, "Asian Performance Tradition and Contemporary Cultural Reality")

Is theatre a business? Is theatre an art? Can theatre be both art and business? If so, what is the proper relationship between business and theatre? If not, how can theatre survive separate from business? These are basic questions that dominate a great many real-life conversations among people who make their livelihood working in the theatre. They arise whenever theatre people talk about what has happened to theatre in the United States during this century, and what is happening now. As common as the theatre-as-art-and/or-business subject is, I have yet to read a theatre history textbook that addresses economic issues in any significant way.

As I write in January 1997, the League of Resident Theatres, which is the official negotiating body for approximately two hundred regional, professional, not-for-profit theatres in the United States, and United Scenic Artists, the labor union that represents most theatre designers whose primary occupation is designing for the professional theatre, are resuming contract negotiations, which have been stalled for several weeks. In a letter dated December 26, 1996, and addressed to all LORT artistic directors, managing directors, and boards of directors concerning these negotiations, scene designer Ming Cho Lee discusses the connections between theatre art and theatre business:

> It is with great sadness that I have learned that the negotiations between USA Local 829 and LORT have been broken off. I have had a long-standing relationship with the LORT theatres, and have been designing for them since the beginning of the resident theatre movement. . . . I have spoken out publicly at Congressional hearings and at colleges and universities on the importance of the resident theatres. I have always treated my work at the resident theatres

> as an end in itself, and have never considered it a stepping stone for some other seemingly more glamorous or lucrative job. . . . I consider resident theatre to be my artistic and professional home. . . .
>
> . . . The ugly reality that confronts these particular negotiations is the fact that on one hand, the LORT theatres are currently facing unprecedented financial constraints, and are fighting for their very survival. At the same time, it is equally true that the designers are not only unable to earn even a minimally respectable living working for LORT theatres, but are frequently not even breaking even. . . .
>
> . . . I [feel] strongly that LORT should at least begin to consider the concept of per diem for designers. . . . The amount of time that a costume designer is required to stay out of town in order to fulfill his/her responsibility is often overwhelming, and the financial burden of such a stay should be recognized and be compensated one way or the other. . . .
>
> . . . I would like to first remind everyone that almost all the designers working for LORT theatres have been working in good faith, and have contributed to the standard of their productions; and not only are we not making a living from the work, but quite often we are contributing our money and time in order to make the design and production possible. . . .
>
> . . . We must reopen the negotiations without prior conditions *in order to get on with our work. For all of us, this is to do good theatre* [emphasis mine].

Unlike painters and poets, who can do their work alone in studios and studies, theatre designers must, at the very least, have a couple of colleagues with whom to collaborate and for whom to design. Eventually, theatre designers need not only a group of performers but physical theatres with stages and electricity, and craftspeople to help them turn their ideas into realities. When all these elements come together for the express purpose of making live theatre for live audiences, we call it a theatre company. Somewhere along the organizational path, a theatre company turns into a business.

Increasingly in recent years, theatre designers have come to realize that in order to succeed in getting their work from page to stage, to "do good theatre," they must make certain connections between art and business. Virtually every professional designer who is hired to design for a contemporary theatre organization signs a formal contract that lists and describes each task for which the designer is responsible. The contract binds the designer to specific dates for design conferences, sketch deadlines, and technical and dress rehearsals, and states the periods of time during which the designer is required to be in residence. A design fee is set forth in the contract and usually the production budget is also included. Upon signing this document, the designer agrees to abide by its contents. It is, in effect, a business agreement between the designer and the theatre organization for whom the work will be done.

It is foolish indeed to assume that making theatre today is somehow separate from the business of theatre.

What happens to the art of theatre under contract? Working designers almost never read and analyze playscripts with total objectivity or for an ideal production. As soon as an agreement has been struck, a designer hired, and the work begun, all phases of the design process, including script and text analysis, are done through the combined filters of which company, what physical space, how much time, and how much money. All these considerations may impose a sense of restriction on the design process when, for example, the budget is too small or the time for building and hanging too short. Even when time and budget appear to be adequate, the design process itself is always constrained by dates and deadlines. Almost no one in the United States today sets out to work on a production for as long as it takes to bring it together. The first action of any producing group is to establish a date for their production to open; the second is to announce this date to prospective audiences. These actions are business actions.

What happens to the art of theatre when it must work within limits and on a schedule? Americans, for the most part, approve of business. Art to many Americans is a questionable activity. Our strong, mostly positive feelings about business, and our vague, subtly negative feelings about art are part of our national character. An artist, however, who turns his or her art into a business earns public approval. Should the art-as-business become successful, the artist gains additional respect and is seen not only as an artist who has managed to make art people want to buy, but also as an artist whose work is obviously better than the work of an artist who never earns anything from painting, sculpting, or designing sets for plays. It follows quite naturally that the artist whose business is the most successful becomes, in the public's estimation, not only the richest artist but the best artist. Many would argue to the contrary—that good art and highly profitable art are not one and the same. However, even those of us who are totally opposed to the notion that a theatrical event that succeeds in the marketplace has *ipso facto* proven itself superior to one that sustains only a modest success find ourselves having to struggle constantly with a deep-seated tendency to favor businesslike theatre organizations and productions that are profitable. After all, we can only make good theatre in a well-organized atmosphere that provides a group of trained workers, technical support, and funding. What happens when theatre we believe is good fails to find an audience and does not sell? Who pays to keep the production open? Should it be kept open if it has failed to sell?

How long has this been going on?

Theatre as Business

Between 1856 and 1956, professional theatre in the United States was firmly in the hands of New York producers, theatre owners, and businessmen. At the turn of the century, two organizations dominated the theatrical scene: first, a group of booking agents and theatre owners who came to be called the Syndicate, and later the Shuberts. In 1905, Lee, Sam S., and Jacob J. Shubert took advantage of a new business organizational structure and formed the first corporation to produce a theatrical product. By 1915, the Syndicate had fallen apart and the Schuberts were in control.

Not only did these two organizations in turn control most of the theatre seen in New York, they also controlled touring productions. During the last half of the nineteenth century, the Syndicate built such a strong nationwide booking monopoly that it was able to decide which plays would tour and which actors would appear in the productions. Naturally enough, it chose noncontroversial plays that were popular star vehicles and had mass audience appeal. The Shuberts managed to take over the theatrical touring market from the Syndicate by buying or building their own theatres all across the country. After the Syndicate's demise, the Shuberts continued to control national touring until 1956, when they were found in violation of antitrust legislation and forced to sell many of their theatres. Theatre touring virtually stopped during the years of the Great Depression and for the duration of World War II. When national tours resumed after the war, they bypassed the small and medium-sized cities that had provided such eager audiences until 1929 and played only in the largest metropolitan areas. Vast areas of the United States had no access whatsoever to live professional theatre. From the 1930s until the 1960s, when most Americans talked about American theatre they meant New York theatre, and primarily Broadway.

Theatre as Art

During the same period—from the mid-nineteenth century through the mid-twentieth—Western theatre as art experienced many changes. There was philosophical and critical debate about the proper content of drama, conflict over form, a great deal of experimentation with performance techniques, and explosive new approaches to theatre design. Strong, articulate personalities made their appearance in every theatrical area, creating more than a little inherent drama. Unfortunately for theatre in the United States, virtually all the early action took place across the Atlantic, and it was not until the 1920s that European ideas had any significant influence on the American theatre.

Lively arguments about the nature of art in general and theatre in particular were taking place in England and Europe at the end of the nineteenth century. Is theatre actually an art form in and of itself or is it merely an assemblage of individual art forms? Must theatre be a business? Can a theatre that operates like a business also be art? Who is ultimately responsible for creating a theatrical event? Does theatre have a mission and if so what is it? (Does it surprise you that we are asking the very same questions at the end of this century?)

This is the period during which Realism was born and the plays of Strindberg, Ibsen, Chekhov, and Shaw were both admired and deplored in the theatres of England and Europe. By the 1880s, Stephane Mallarmé, a symbolist poet who also wrote poetic dramas and dramatic criticism, was claiming that there was already too much realism in the theatre and calling for a "higher form" of drama. Symbolism was only one of the many "isms" that made up the antirealism movement, and all were also associated with movements in the other arts, especially painting and poetry. Symbolism, expressionism, futurism, dadaism, and surrealism all had their hour upon the stage, and even though few of the plays written exclusively in these modes seem as potent today as they were in their own time, and for their own audiences, each in its own way exerted a strong influence on twentieth-century playwriting and production. None of these movements produced commercially viable plays for the U.S. market, however, and the only Americans who saw what we might now call experimental drama were those who traveled abroad.

The New Stagecraft

> Edward Gordon Craig and Robert Edmund Jones are the designers I feel have influenced me the most. It's interesting to me that those two designers pop up so easily in my head, for their approach to the stage space itself is as scenic artists, and I'm primarily a costume designer. Their work continually rears its head in my costume design, however. The sharp, simple silhouette and the contrast of the straight line moving with and against the human form intrigues me. (Jamie Bullins, theatre designer)

Two of the most challenging voices that called for a total reform in theatre design and production methods during this period were Adolphe Appia (1862–1928), born in Geneva, and Edward Gordon Craig (1872–1966), a Londoner. Prior to the design innovations in which these two men participated, and which came to be known as the New Stagecraft, theatre sets served primarily as backdrops for the actors, and there was little visual relationship between the scenery and the human form. Painted perspective scenery was beautiful in itself, but it isolated the actor, who remained the same size and within the same visual plane on the forestage, in front of, not within the receding scene. Traditional box sets contained separate, usually unrelated visual elements: walls, floor, stationary items such as furniture, and moving actors.

Adolphe Appia perceived that his greatest design challenge was to create a relationship between the moving human being, the horizontal floor, and the vertical scenery. Most designers, who were at that time largely painters, thought of scenery as something "back there," behind and partly around the actors. Appia imagined the set as a completely unified space, an "in here."

> One of my friends at the boarding school had seen *Tannhäuser* in Germany and gave me vague reports of it. I tried to pin him down and inquired whether the characters were really "in a place" and what this "place" looked like. He did not understand me. I remember having been rather insistent and having finally asked almost in despair: "Where were their feet?" To be sure, such preoccupation is characteristic of a fourteen-year-old boy; I am now sixty and still greatly concerned about where the actor's feet are. ("Theatrical Experiences and Personal Investigations," 1921)

Appia manipulated volume and mass. He shaped the stage space with platforms, ramps, and steps, and with three-dimensional pillars and drapes, and made the actor a central element of the design. As the actor moved through the set, vertically as well as horizontally, the actor's body created the element of rhythm that unified the whole. Appia said: "Our body is the expression of space in time and time in space." He called the theatre a "cathedral" and believed that the central emotional experience of theatre was possible because the audience was living the play as it happened.

Fortunately, Appia was a prolific and articulate writer. Along with essays on designing performance spaces that include rather than isolate the audience, stagecraft that focuses on the human actor, and the relationship between designers and text, Appia was one of the first to explore what have become the basic ideas of modern stage lighting theory.

> Lighting is an element in itself whose effects are limitless; set free, it becomes for us what his palette is for the painter; all combinations of color can be created with it. By means of simple or complex, fixed or moving, projections—by justified obstructions, by diverse degrees of transparency, etc.,—we can achieve infinite modulations. Thus by means of light we can in a way materialize colors and forms, which are immobilized on painted canvas, and can bring them alive in space. No longer does the actor walk in front of painted shadows and highlights; he is plunged into an atmosphere that is uniquely his own. Artists will easily understand the extent of such a reform. ("Ideas on a Reform of Our *Mise en Scene*" c. 1902)

Three-dimensional scenery and three-dimensional actors appear flat under the kind of general illumination stage lighting that ushered in this century. Appia designed lighting positions that allowed him to bring light in from many directions, which deepened the shapes on the stage by means of contrast. He was perhaps the first theatre designer to use light to "sculpt" the stage space. Light, he said, was like music and it was his primary means of harmonizing all the visual elements on the stage. Because he focused on the effects of light and shadow, Appia rendered his designs in shades of black and white.

Edward Gordon Craig's mother was the famous actress Ellen Terry, and he began his theatrical career as an actor. Soon he began to direct and design productions in England, Germany, and Denmark. Craig was far more flamboyant and outspoken than Appia. Because he had little success trying to persuade the "hidebound" English theatre to change its too-traditional ways, he mounted a continuous, sometimes outrageous verbal tirade. He was opinionated, difficult, and brilliant. Craig's reputation, and his subsequent influence on twentieth-century theatre, comes largely from his books: *The Art of the Theatre*, 1905; *On the Art of the Theatre*, 1911; *Towards a New Theatre*, 1913; *The Theatre Advancing*, 1919; and his magazine, *The Mask*, which he published off and on from 1908 to 1929. Craig's scene design drawings provide dramatic illustrations for his ideas, but most of them were never meant to be designs for actual productions.

Craig insisted that theatre has the potential to be an art as fine and as pure as music, painting, or poetry. He maintained that the theatre of his own day, however, was not an art, and he was convinced it would never be an art until all its ragtag elements—actors, designers, playwrights, technicians, and so on—surrendered themselves to the superior vision and firm guiding hand of a master craftsman, or artist stage director (a role in which Craig certainly saw himself!). Craig called this super-director "the theatre artist" of the coming era:

> If the stage director was to technically train himself for his task of interpreting the plays of the dramatist—in time, and by a gradual development he would again recover the ground lost to the theatre, and finally would restore the Art of the Theatre to its home by means of his own creative genius. ("The First Dialogue," *The Art of the Theatre*)

Craig's director/dictator, who must "rule on the stage," creates a personal vision of what the play should mean, and how it should look. Ideally, he or she is sufficiently strong and seductive to make sure the actors and designers do what this personal vision demands. Craig's ideas about who should create the Art of the Theatre significantly influenced how theatre directors defined their work during most of this century. His ideas, which were adopted by other writers and widely circulated, also had a profound effect on the relationship between directors and designers, establishing an intellectual hierarchy that has done a great deal of damage to the collaborative process in theatre, and from which we are only just beginning to emerge.

With few exceptions, commercial theatre in the United States during the first quarter of this century had no interest whatsoever in the New Stagecraft, or in any kind of play that could be described by a word ending in "ism." New kinds of plays and new approaches to production and design were introduced to American audiences by noncommercial theatre companies, which were part of the Little Theatre Movement, and by way of performances given on college and university campuses. The little theatres and the campus dramatic associations were made up of amateurs and academics who were committed to the art of theatre rather than to theatre as a profitable product.

Many of those who worked in noncommercial American theatre at this time had been inspired by productions they had seen in England and on the continent. By 1915, there was a large enough art theatre audience for Granville Barker, the principal director of the London's Royal Court Theatre, to mount an entire season in New York, including plays by the controversial playwright George Bernard Shaw. Also in 1915, Americans had their first look at examples of the New Stagecraft in an exhibit mounted by the American designer Sam Hume, which included works by Appia and Craig.

By 1917, when Sheldon Cheney founded *Theatre Arts Magazine*, a journal that served as a focus for new theatre ideas, there were approximately fifty little theatres, sometimes called art theatres, operating in America. The most influential of the little theatres either began or ended up in New York. The list includes:

> *The Provincetown Playhouse*, which began in Provincetown, Massachusetts in 1915 and moved to Greenwich Village in 1916, is remembered chiefly as the first producer of Eugene O'Neill's plays.
>
> *The Neighborhood Playhouse*, founded at about the same time by two wealthy, well-educated, widely traveled sisters, Irene and Alice Lewisohn, was noted for beautiful, unified productions of largely noncommercial plays, and later became one of America's major professional theatre schools.
>
> *The Washington Square Players* only operated from 1915 to 1918 but several of the group's members went on to found *The Theatre Guild*, which was the first financially successful producer of "alternative" plays in the United States. The mission statement of The Theatre Guild said, in part, that it intended "to produce plays of artistic merit not ordinarily produced by the commercial managers."

The activities of all these groups, as well as others across the country, were either ended or severely curtailed by the disastrous economic effects of the Great Depression.

The Federal Theatre

Hallie Flanagan began her theatrical career in the noncommercial theatre and received her formal training as a student of George Pierce Baker, considered the father of theatre education in the United States. In 1903, he began teaching a class in playwriting at Radcliffe College. Shortly thereafter, this course was opened to Harvard students and, ten years later, Baker added a production workshop to his English 47 Workshop. Among the more famous students in Baker's workshop were Eugene O'Neill, Thomas Wolfe, Sidney Howard, Robert Edmond Jones, Lee Simonson, George Abbott, Philip Barry, Samuel Hume, and Hallie Flanagan. Dozens of other students, less well known by name, studied with Baker and fanned out across the country to carry his message to a new generation of aspiring writers, performers, and designers. In the 1930s, Yale University invited Baker to develop a program of study devoted specifically to theatre, and he moved to New Haven to found the Yale Drama School.

Hallie Flanagan began her studies with George Pierce Baker in 1923. Two years earlier, she had heard Baker speak at Grinnell College in Grinnell, Iowa, where she was teaching English and directing plays, both at the college and at the local little theatre. She remembered him saying that drama could be a force in modern life just as it had been for the ancient Greeks. Hallie Flanagan shared this belief. She spent a year in Cambridge, Massachusetts, and the following year on a European study tour, for which she was awarded a Guggenheim Fellowship. During her study tour, she went to the theatre in every country she visited and met with playwrights, actors, directors, and designers, including Meyerhold and Edward Gordon Craig. When she returned she was offered a teaching position at Vassar College. A biographer, Jane Bentley, writes:

> If any of the thirty-five girls who gathered in the Avery Hall greenroom for their first class with Hallie in the fall of 1927 thought that the course was going to be easy, they soon learned otherwise. Hallie entered the greenroom carrying Craig's *On the Art of the Theatre* and Stanislavsky's *My Life in Art*. She placed these books and a red alarm clock on a small round table in the room's center. Student chairs were arranged in a semicircle facing her. Several students had heard that Hallie was an inspiring teacher, and some had decided they were not going to be impressed. But when Hallie began to speak, the room became instantly still. "She could command an audience

> just by the tone of her voice," was one recollection. Hallie discussed her idea of theatre. It could bring people together, change their ideas, and enlarge their way of looking at the world. The Greeks had known the power of theatre, so had the English of Shakespeare's day, but America was only now getting to know it. Although Broadway was still doing old-fashioned scripts in old-fashioned ways, American audiences were beginning to demand something more. A new theatre had emerged in Europe and was emerging in Russia. Hallie talked about Craig, Stanislavsky, and Meyerhold and sent her students off to the library to read about expressionism, impressionism, and constructivism. Within weeks she had fired most of them with an enthusiasm approaching her own. (*Hallie Flanagan, A Life in the American Theatre*)

The Federal Theatre was part of President Franklin Roosevelt's Works Progress Administration (WPA), a network of government-sponsored programs to provide work for the millions who were without jobs as a result of

Figure 6–1. *Hallie Flanagan Davis, director of the Federal Theatre. Photograph courtesy of the National Archives.*

Figure 6–2. *Scene from the Federal Theatre's* Living Newspaper *production,* "... one-third of a nation ...," *New York, 1938. Photograph courtesy of the National Archives.*

the Great Depression. Hallie Flanagan Davis (she had married Greek scholar, Philip Davis, in 1934) took the oath of office as director of the Federal Theatre on August 27, 1935. Her immediate job was to put ten thousand theatre people to work. Her personal and professional goal was the formation of a national theatre, with companies in every state, which would survive the Depression and provide a foundation for the future of the American theatre.

The Federal Theatre was, from the beginning, the target of bitter political attacks by members of Congress who opposed the Emergency Relief Appropriation Act of 1935 in general, and the production of controversial, argumentative, and thought-provoking theatre at the taxpayers' expense in particular. The rhetoric of these attacks is astonishingly similar to the verbal barrage aimed at the National Endowment for the Arts in the 1980s and 1990s

Figure 6–3. *Audience in Peoria Heights, Illinois, watching the Federal Tent Theatre production of* Mississippi Rainbow, *July 1937. Photograph courtesy of the National Archives.*

by conservative members of Congress. The Federal Theatre was terminated on June 30, 1939, when Congress dropped it from the funding bill. Malcolm Cowley lamented its demise in an issue of *The New Republic* in 1941:

> In the first place, it [the Federal Theatre] provided steady work for eight thousand penniless theatrical people. That was its primary purpose, under the law setting up the WPA, and was quite enough to justify the money spent on the project. But in the second place, it also brought stage shows, at a low price or none at all, to people who were starved for entertainment and in many cases had never seen a living actor. It gave regional pageants, comedies specially written to be played in the barracks of CCC camps, tent shows, marionette plays for children and Living Newspapers for the broad public; and much of what it did was tied up with the daily lives of people watching the performance. The Federal Theatre was creating an entirely

new audience, just as free libraries had created a new audience for books; that explains why the commercial theatre tried hard to defend it later, when it was being attacked in Congress. And in the third place, it produced an astonishing number of good plays, old and new, highbrow and popular, everything from Marlowe and Shakespeare to surrealism and "The Swing Mikado." It was for a time the center of almost everything that was fresh and experimental on the American stage. More than that, it came closer than anything else we have had—perhaps closer than anything we shall get in the future—to being an American national theatre.

Not-for-Profit Theatre and the NEA

Throughout the history of the theatre, as of the arts in general, support for theatrical events, when they are recognized as an integral part of the social structure rather than a profit-making product, has been provided by ruling families, civic organizations, and governments. The long history of governmental involvement with the arts began in 534 B.C., when the Athenian government accorded official sanction and financial support to the theatre. The relationship between government and the arts has been fraught with difficulty over the centuries as governments have grappled with the opinions of the citizenry on what constitutes art and the artists who make it. Today, every developed nation in the world has, at the cabinet level of its government, an agency—a ministry of culture, for instance—with oversight for the preservation of the arts, antiquities, and way of life of the country's people. Except the United States. In many countries, the work of artists, including theatre artists, is so revered by their citizens that artists and arts organizations are subsidized by the government.

Until the creation of the Federal Theatre in 1935 as part of an emergency public works program, government funding of the arts in the United States was limited to memorial statues and military bands. After 1939 and the demise of the Federal Theatre, the American theatre returned to business as usual.

A bit more than ten years later, Arena Stage in Washington, D.C. opened as a profit-seeking corporation, a business. The intent of the corporation, however, under the artistic directorship of Zelda Fichandler, was to produce serious theatre art, not simply entertainment. During its first year of operation, Arena Stage offered seventeen productions, all of which played to respectably full

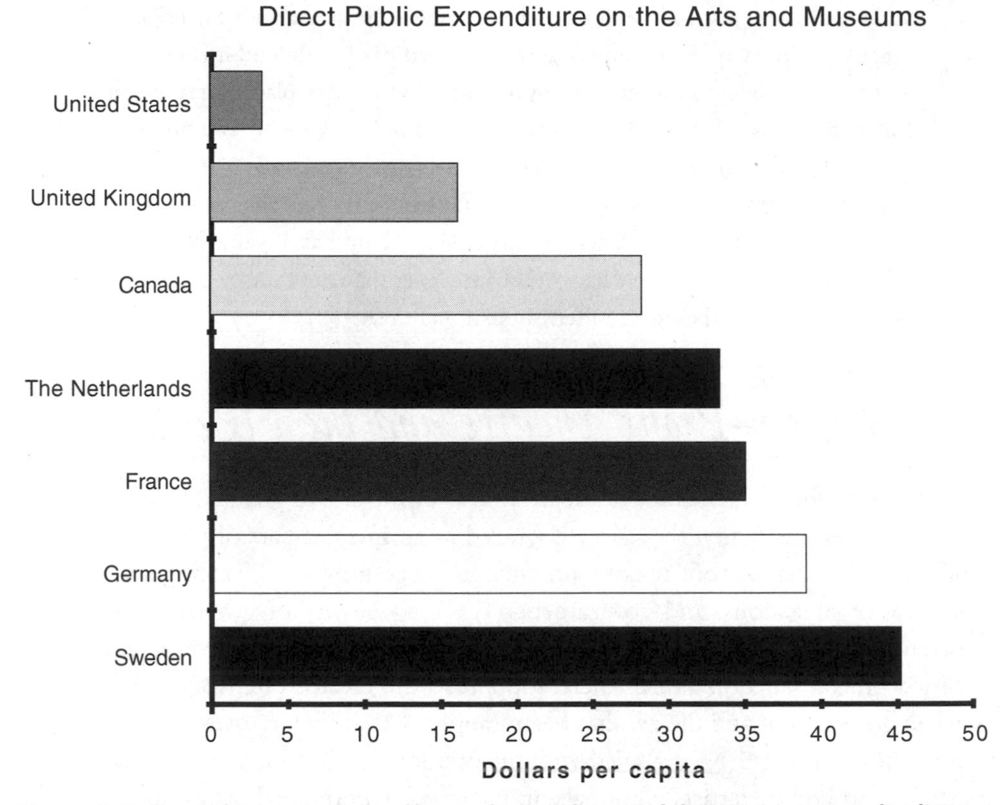

Figure 6–4. *Bar graph comparing direct public expenditure on the arts, including museums, among selected Western nations. Chart courtesy of the National Endowment for the Arts.*

houses and received enthusiastic critical response. Making serious art is labor-intensive, however, and at the end of the year there was no profit. As a result of this frustrating effort, Zelda Fichandler became one of the first artistic directors in the country to propose that theatre contributes to culture in ways similar to schools, art museums, and libraries. She sought and obtained a not-for-profit status for Arena Stage. This enabled the organization to accept tax-deductible donations that allowed their work to continue. Other theatres were also granted the not-for-profit status, and a new era in American theatre began.

A further ten years passed before there was any serious discussion of direct government involvement in the arts. In the early 1960s, studies carried out by the Rockefeller Foundation and the economic firm of Baumol & Bowen resulted in reports supporting what so many struggling producers of serious,

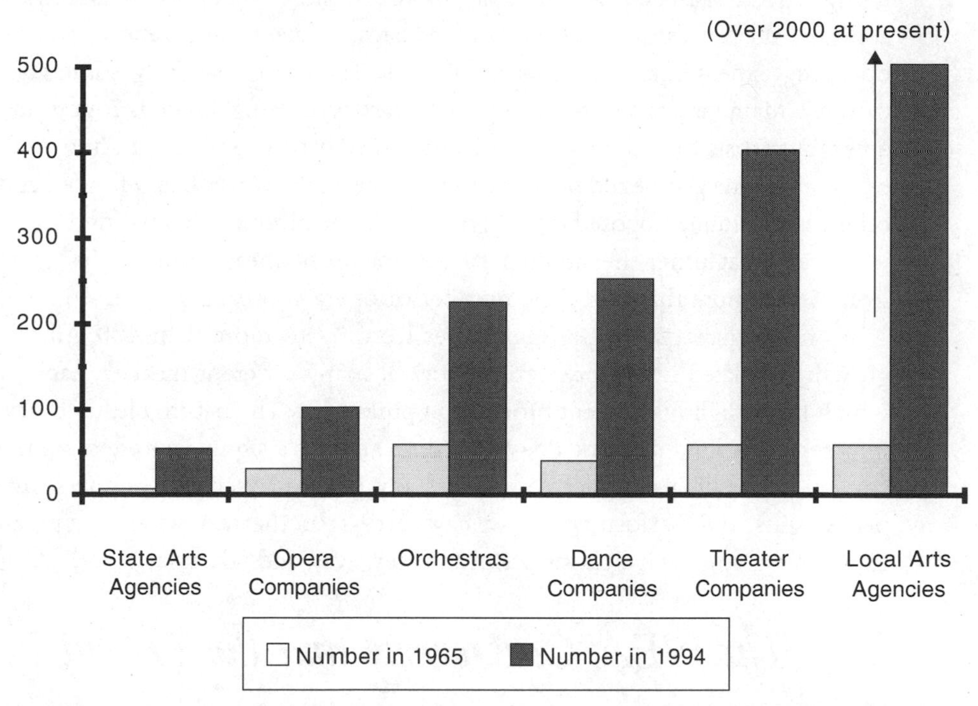

Figure 6–5. *Bar graph illustrating the growth of arts organizations in the United States from the establishment of the National Endowment for the Arts in 1965 through 1994. Chart courtesy of the National Endowment for the Arts.*

noncommercial theatre already knew from experience: serious art in the United States could never be financially solvent without government support. The Rockefeller Report emphasized the labor-intensive nature of all the arts and pointed out that there is no way to substitute for people in making art.

As a result, and with the urging of President Lyndon Johnson, the U.S. Congress authorized the creation of the National Endowment for the Arts in 1965. The mission of the Endowment is

- to foster the excellence, diversity, and vitality of the arts in the U.S.
- to broaden the availability of that excellence, diversity, and vitality;
- and, in order to achieve the above, award grants to professional artists and non-profit arts organizations who have a proven track record of excellence.

From 1965 until 1989, the National Endowment for the Arts succeeded in doing what it had been created to do: more art, more audiences, greater availability of the arts throughout the United States, efficient organization, sensible operating expenses, and no internal scandals. There was, naturally, some controversy. Many artists felt that only "safe" art was being funded. Young and emerging artists fretted because only established artists received funding. And, of course, some people did not approve of some of the works being funded and others were simply opposed to any government involvement in arts funding.

During that time, the number of not-for-profit theatre companies grew from 56 to more than 600. The number of opera companies increased from 27 to more than 120; dance companies from 37 to more than 400. All this growth translated into more design work at many different theatres, each of which has a slightly different production philosophy. The nature of the theatre influences the kind of work a designer does and has a significant effect on the context in which a designer approaches any given playscript. Designers, like playwrights and performers, now have access to theatres where they can experiment, approach a classic script in a new way, and take risks.

The NEA Controversy and the Present

> Theatre plays a unique and critical role in society. Our artists often ask the questions that others find too terrifying, explore topics that some find unmentionable and seek to right injustice that many would rather ignore. For these reasons our work today is as it has been for centuries, and will be forever, dangerous to members of our world who fear its truth and impact. Because the performance of dramatic literature has the power to change people's lives, we need to be ever-vigilant in our mindful watch of the government's attempts to silence the voices of our artists. (Gregg Stull, teacher and director)

Now we come to the series of events that initiated the alterations in the theatre workplace designers began to feel in the mid-1990s. Naturally, no shift in human affairs is caused by a single element alone—attitudes change, young organizations become mature institutions, the economy alters, political pressures are felt—all a long time before something happens that appears to change everything. The relatively secure world of not-for-profit theatre, and the comforting presence of the National Endowment for the Arts, however, does seem to have begun to crumble overnight.

The inciting incidents were exhibits by two visual artists, one in North Carolina, the other scheduled to open in Washington, D.C., which contained images a member of the House of Representatives labeled "morally reprehensible trash." Overnight the NEA became the object of intense attacks, which continue. NEA opponents do not take into consideration that the organization has awarded over 110,000 grants to thousands of American artists and arts organizations in all fifty states, and that less than forty have been considered controversial in any way. Obviously the offending images only served to jump-start a reaction against direct government involvement in the arts that had been simmering all along. The national mood has become more conservative and no matter how many cars and computers we own, we do not feel as prosperous as we did a dozen years ago. Finger-pointing and "downsizing" are in the air. The arts are an easy target.

Many members of Congress have stated that it is their intention to phase out federal funding for the National Endowment for the Arts over a two-year period beginning in 1997. Indeed, by the time this book appears, the NEA, like the Federal Theatre, may be a matter of history. Funding has already been cut from $162,311,000 to $99,494,000 between 1995 and 1996. In addition, Congress plans to take a close look at organizations that have been awarded the not-for-profit status and to withdraw that status from groups that do not meet some as yet unstated standards.

The situation today's designer faces is the combined result of federal funding cuts, associated reductions in private donations, rising material and labor costs, and skyrocketing ticket prices. At the same time, the NEA controversy has reawakened dormant negative feelings about art that seem always to lurk in the sensibilities of many Americans and have caused audiences to be less open to disturbing, challenging theatre. As a result of all these combined forces some theatres have closed, some have decreased the number and the character of the productions they offer, many have reduced the number of regular company members, and all have shortened their rehearsal and construction periods.

Why should theatre designers be concerned, particularly when these issues and events seem so far beyond our control? The answer is that we must be concerned, because the alternative is to give up our voices as well as our workplace. More important, it is to refuse to participate in redesigning the theatre in which we will continue to work. Today's designers are responsible in part for tomorrow's theatre. Here are some things you can do:

- Carry out each design project with a conscious awareness of when, where, and for whom you are working. Place your work on a theatrical continuum.
- Read what Adolphe Appia, Edward Gordon Craig, and Robert Edmond Jones have written about theatre design and study their work.
- Find out about Hallie Flanagan's vision for the Federal Theatre, and read a script from *The Living Newspaper* series.
- Pay attention to what is happening in theatre today, in the United States and elsewhere. Read well beyond the Arts and Entertainment sections of the newspaper in order to discover how business and political events are affecting theatre.
- Develop your own personal notion of an ideal theatre that can inspire you to do your best work. Imagine it. Foster that image in every design project you undertake.

The Audience

7

Theatre, unlike the more static arts, presents a number of classic paradoxes:

> It is unique to the moment, yet it is repeatable.
> It is spontaneous, yet it is rehearsed.
> It is participatory, yet it is presented.
> It is real, yet it is simulated.
> It is understandable, yet it is obscure.
> The actors are themselves, yet they are characters.
> The audience believes, yet it does not believe.
> The audience is involved, yet it remains apart.
>
> Robert Cohen, *Theatre*

All of us, beginning in infancy and continuing throughout our lives, have an instinct for imitating or representing the actions, activities, and behaviors we observe and imagine. This instinct is the foundation for all kinds of performances. Fortunately for the instinctive performer in us all, we also come equipped with the capacity to enjoy imitation, plus the curiosity and interest to seek it out. Audiences are groups of people who enjoy watching performances together. These natural propensities to imitate and to enjoy imitation were described by Aristotle in the fourth century B.C. in *The Poetics*, our oldest book of dramatic theory, which has quite a lot to say about audiences. Because imitation comes naturally to individuals, all human societies throughout history and in every part of the world make theatre.

Here is a working definition of the word *theatre* as it is used to mean the peculiar kind of theatrical event that satisfies our human instinct for imitation and our desire to participate in imitative experiences: *Theatre describes a wide range of planned, or scripted, events, in which a live performer, or performers, imitates, or represents, a character, or characters, with, or in front of, a live audience.* In this sense, theatre in its broadest interpretation encompasses performances of all kinds of plays, skits, pageants, pantomimes, musicals, operas, dances, and combinations of the above; it does not mean a filmed, videotaped, or computerized product, fixed and unchanging, that we can watch alone or with other watchers. Theatre, for our purposes, is a participatory event related much more closely to a religious ritual, a pep rally, or a political demonstration than to watching a feature film in a movie house or a situation comedy on television. Because theatre is live, because it is happening right now, in the present, it has a peculiar power to seem, as Robert Cohen points out, unique, spontaneous, participatory, and downright real.

Official and Unofficial Theatre

If time travel were possible and we could visit Athens in the fifth century B.C., Wakefield, England, in the fourteenth century, London in 1600, Paris in 1784, or indeed, any other theatre-rich time in the history of Western civilization, we would hear and see many more kinds of theatrical events in progress than our theatre history textbooks would lead us to expect. In fact, the kinds of theatre being done in ancient Greece or Elizabethan England might be very much like the kinds of theatre being done in the United States, England, and Europe in the 1990s, including, in part:

- young people creating and attending plays based on familiar stories, often with positive moral and ethical content
- a community dramatizing its founding or an important event in its history
- slapstick comedy performed in the afternoons at fairs, festivals, and weekend outings
- romantic comedies performed in the evenings at the same events
- political skits, most probably in major cities and at times of elections, protests, or political instability
- religious dramas, both inside and outside places of worship

- erotic representations, generally pricey
- "professional" theatre companies performing scheduled productions of "official" and possibly licensed works of past and current playwrights, presented at regular intervals for audiences that might include everybody in town or a selective, often affluent, minority

When we study theatre history, however, we concentrate on official theatre—the plays, playwrights, and types of performance that were most acceptable to and often licensed by the political, social, and intellectual establishment of the time—and, of necessity, on the playscripts preserved, often deliberately, by people or organizations who have decided they were worth saving. The scripts for street-corner political satire, religious playlets, and bicentennial celebrations disappear, and in general very few records or descriptions of these productions ever survive.

Of the official playscripts that are saved, copied, printed, and published, the ones that are widely read and often revived tend to be those that speak to universal human issues: the relationship between the human and the divine; people's responsibility for one another; the role of government in human society; war; the constructive and destructive powers of love, sex, and family; and so on. We generally neglect and even forget plays about minor historical incidents and purely local events, or those that take place against a background of such specific lifestyles that audiences unfamiliar with them find the play difficult to follow.

Literary scholars and critics have a hand in choosing which plays make it into anthologies and onto library shelves, and thus which ones are available for study. Critics focus on plays with established literary status, plays that adhere to a recognized form, read well on the page, and are perceived to have value as literature apart from performance, and on influential plays and playwrights, work that often viewed after the fact appears to have led other theatre artists in new directions.

The result of our concentration on official, universal, and literary theatre from earlier times is that most of us come away from theatre history and literature studies with the false notion that far fewer plays were written and produced in past centuries than we can plainly see are being written and produced today, and that there used to be far less theatrical variety than we know is occurring now. Our habit of accepting official theatre history as the *only* theatre history blinds us to the fact that most theatrical events in any period were uninteresting or unacceptable to the political, social, and/or intellectual establishment, were ignored by the critics, then and now, and finally got lost.

Fortunately, our view of theatre history, indeed of all history, has been changing for a good many years. During the last half of this century, we have grown increasingly interested in social history, cultural anthropology, and related fields of study. Today the lives and experiences of ordinary people, minorities, and other marginalized groups are often considered as important to an understanding of human history as the traditional version of history, which focuses on political leaders and geopolitical events, generals and war, captains of industry and economics. Our view of history is shifting away from the idea that great forces shape civilization from the top down to the notion that society is a complex organism in which even the smallest component has a voice and a function, and affects the behavior of the whole. Researchers everywhere are combing through letters and diaries, broadsides, newspapers and journals, civic and organizational records, popular literature and popular entertainment, reaching as far back into history as we can go, in order to inject new material into, and take a new look at, traditional history and official sources. Not infrequently, this new information, coming from people whose life experiences differed significantly from kings, governors, generals, the wealthy, and the well educated, has altered the official accepted version. Our knowledge of theatre history has been greatly enriched by the work of historians, anthropologists, geographers, linguists, and many others who have ventured beyond official sources to find out what people like ourselves were thinking and doing, what their hopes and expectations were, and how the world looked from unofficial points of view.

Quilters, a recent play that never fails to delight audiences, is based in large part on documents once considered unofficial and therefore overlooked by professional historians. In writing their play, Barbara Damashek and Molly Newman drew, in part, on personal accounts of the westward migration by pioneer women, who recorded their experiences in diaries and letters.

The long-standing official story of America's great nineteenth-century journey, the Westward Expansion, was written by men. This narrative focused on adventure, luck, bravery, fights with Indians, and the noble quest for land, gold, independence, and prosperity. Although half of the pioneers were women, their story was an unofficial whisper for nearly a hundred years. When women's voices were finally granted a place in the historical record, the official story began to change: Indians become guides and trading partners as often as they were enemies; the treks were actually longer and more monotonous; many more died of accident, snakebite, dysentery, and cholera than previous accounts had recorded. The following section from Lillian Schlissel's *Women's Diaries of the Westward Journey* illustrates the contrast between the ways pioneer men and women recorded death on their Westward journey.

> In another aspect the women's diaries differ from the diaries written by men. As ritual caretakers of the sick and the dying, the women saw the real enemies of the road as disease and accident. It is in the women's diaries that we are reminded that the heaviest emigration of the Overland Trail was accomplished during years of cholera epidemic. As travelers hurried across the continent to the "rag towns" of California and Nevada in order to pan the clear streams for gold, cholera swept over the Trail.
>
> Nowhere in the world could it have been more bleak to be stricken than on an open and unmarked road, to be left by the side of the Trail either to recover or to die. The women write of the deaths and the burials. They tell of typhoid, mountain fever, measles, dysentery and drownings. The women knew that disease and accident killed more emigrants than did Indians. The women, whose job it was to care for the dying, carefully noted the cost of the westward movement in human life. Whereas men recorded the death in aggregate numbers, the women knew death as personal catastrophe and noted the particulars of each grave site, whether it was newly dug or old, whether of a young person or an adult, whether it had been disturbed by wolves or by Indians. The women were the actuaries of the road, tallying the miles with the lives that were lost.

Quilters has been produced all across the country during the past several years in not-for-profit regional theatres, on college and university campuses, and by community theatres. The combination of songs, stories, scenes, and monologues is uniquely dramatic, and most producing groups report that their productions of *Quilters* have been both artistically and financially successful. "Audiences love the play."

Alive and Now

> The only theatre worth saving, the only theatre worth having, is a theatre motion pictures cannot touch. When we succeed in eliminating from it every trace of the photographic attitude of mind, when we succeed in making a production that is the exact antithesis of a motion picture, a production that is everything a motion picture is not and nothing a motion picture is, the old lost magic will return once more. The realistic theatre, we may remember, is less than a hundred years old. But the theatre—great theatre, world theatre—is far older than that, so many centuries older that by comparison it makes our little candid-camera theatre seem like something that was thought up only the day before yesterday. We need not be impatient. A brilliant fresh theatre will presently appear. (Robert Edmond Jones, *The Dramatic Imagination*)

Theatre (as we have defined it) is different from a film or a televised production in two crucial ways:

1. The performers are alive and present in the playing space, and the audience is alive and present in the looking place.
2. The performance is occurring in the present, and the audience is experiencing the performance in the present.

Each theatrical event actually happens only once. It is, as Robert Cohen says, "unique to the moment." Of course, as Cohen goes on to point out, reflecting the paradoxical nature of theatre, "it is also repeatable."

Theatre is repeatable in much the same way religious rituals are: the script of the ritual is constant and the officiators are the same for each celebration; but the communication between a single repetition of the ritual event and the celebrants is a one-time thing. From this perspective, no two Sunday morning Masses are the same, no two Passover meals, no two periods of structured meditation. In the theatre, performers, like priests, present, in Aristotle's words, a representation of "men in action and doing things." Each audience member responds to the representation in ways which are "unique to the moment."

Considering the Audience

The lewdness of comedy could never have been suffered by audiences, unless the customs of society had previously sanctioned the same lewdness. (Cicero, *De Republica*, c. 46 B.C.)

Let me be censured by the austerest brow,
Where I want art, or judgment; tax me freely:
Let envious censors, with their broadest eyes,
Look through, and through me, I pursue no favor.
Only vouchsafe me your attentions,
And I will give you music worth your ears.
(Ben Jonson, *Every Man Out of His Humour*, 1600)

The laws can determine the subjects of the plays, and their form, and the way to play them; but the laws cannot force the public to enjoy them. (Jean-Jacques Rousseau, *Politics and the Arts* 1785)

How often do theatre designers put themselves opposite the stage in the theatre's looking place? How specifically do we consider what effects the play and the specific details of our own work will have, might have, ought to have on the audience? How many of us think about the audience at all in our text analysis process?

Most books about making theatre have little or nothing to say about the audience. A few months ago I spent a day in the library looking for what other writers have said about theatre audiences. I pulled out books on directing, acting, designing, theatre history, and dramatic literature. I chose randomly and opened to the table of contents and to the index in each book. As my search for audience progressed, I began to feel as though I was looking for the proverbial needle in the haystack. These are my briefly researched, thoroughly unscientific findings.

1. None of the books contained an entire chapter devoted in any way to theatre audiences.
2. There was no indexed reference to audience in any of the books I examined in the areas of acting, theatre design, or dramatic literature and criticism.

3. Each of the theatre history books had references to *audience* in the index, but when I sampled the specific pages cited, I discovered that nowhere was the audience discussed as an integral part of the theatrical experience. These books regard audiences as rather necessary, somewhat shadowy, usually passive but occasionally obstructive observers. There are references to French, German, and Greek audiences, to illiterate, mass, and medieval audiences, to spectators and to playgoers. Few of the textual references I found were more than a sentence in length.
4. Half of the books on directing included *audience* in the index. The message of all but one of the referenced passages was to remind directors to make their productions appealing to audiences in order to have audiences. The exception to this casually dismissive attitude toward the audience is *Play Directing*, by Francis Hodge.

In chapter 13, "Communication put to work: scene practice and diagnostic criticism," Hodge explains how a performance affects an audience:

> [H]ere is the process: a playwright imagines an improvisation and gives it form through his use of given circumstances, dialogue, dramatic action, characters, idea, moods, tempos; a director then reimagines and recaptures the improvisation; he [the director] then helps the actors and designers to discover the improvisation he sees and feels in the way he sees and feels it, and to recreate it through themselves, thus giving it intensive personal life; if the images they create are strong enough and appropriate enough, the improvisation will be projected in such a way that viewers can receive it and act on it by reimprovising what they have seen and heard *in their own terms* (vicarious experience). Thus, a play is not an object transferred in a direct way but a series of improvisations capable of producing images and, consequently, strong feelings. In this sense, it can be said that a play hovers in space between the stage (playwright, director, actors, designers) and the audience, with the latter receiving it only if it has been released in terms the audience can understand.

This passage is thoughtful and perceptive. Unfortunately, in the context of his whole book, Francis Hodge assigns the director sole responsibility for interpreting the play "in the way he sees and feels it" and controlling its realization "in terms the audience can understand." But I believe that the job of creating lines of comunication between the production and the audience belongs as much to theatre designers as it does to directors. When all members of the production team acknowledge the fact that reaching audiences is as important as creating a production and, from the beginning of the process, explore the ways in which audience connections are going to be made, each facet of the theatrical event will reinforce all the others.

In *The Empty Space*, the director Peter Brook suggests a slightly different equation: "In performance, the relationship is action/subject/audience. In rehearsal it is actor/subject/director. The earliest relationship is director/subject/designer." Although I agree with Brook that the "subject," the play, is always the focus of all theatrical work relationships, I resist the notion of leaving the audience, object of the theatrical event, out of the designer/director equation. Designers have special knowledge about the effects of design on human responses. The predictability of these effects provides the foundation for modern advertising, industrial design, and the interior decor of public as well as private spaces. Fast-food restaurants use reds, oranges, bright white, and long lines culminating in sharp angles to hurry their customers through quick meals and quick departures to make room for new customers. Legend has it that the very successful Notre Dame coach, Knute Rockne, used color theory to win football games. Having heard about the power of color, Rockne painted the locker room used by visiting teams a restful blue-green so they would arrive on the field in a calm, nonaggressive mood. His own team was treated to red-orange walls, which quickened their vital signs and helped send them to a high pitch of excitement. Theatre designers understand the effects of design and can manipulate visual images to make powerful statements. It is an important part of the work. Visual statements, like verbal statements, make little sense out of context. What effects will this play have on its audience? How can I support these effects? emphasize one more than another? expand the effect to encompass a broader meaning? These are some of the questions theatre designers should begin to consider at the very beginning of their playscript and text analyses.

It is crucial, particularly in the early stages of script work, that everyone focus on the play itself rather than on any one person's concept of the play. A production built on the images and ideas of all the collaborators stands a much greater chance of touching most, or even all, of its audience's sensibilities than a so-called conceptual production, which will connect only with audience members who get the concept.

See if you can imagine being able to suggest the richness, the scope, and the ambiguity of the following plays if as a theatre designer your responses to the texts were channeled into the following narrow directorial concepts (from Brian Hansen, *Theatre: The Dynamics of the Art*):

RICHARD III:	A deformed spider crawling across a white robe.
EQUUS:	A medical experiment takes place in an operating amphitheatre while both human beings and gods look on.
MACBETH:	War is a disease; when the war is complete, the fever persists unto madness. Macbeth is a victim of a plague.

Fortunately, the single concept approach to directing and to designing has begun to play itself out, and the doors are open for a fuller and more complete collaboration, which will, I believe, bring us closer to the "brilliant fresh theatre" Robert Edmond Jones imagined back in 1941.

When audiences are one of the primary contexts in which dramatic texts are explored, the theatrical event has the potential to become truly dynamic. In this age of individualism, it is common for all of us to become fixated on the work we do as an expression of our own sensibilities. We often speak of expressing ourselves through our work. Although it is undeniable that all theatre artists do express themselves through their work, the theatrical event in action belongs as much to the audience in the seeing place as it does to those who are in, and who have contributed to the creation of, the playing place. We must also remember that theatre reflects a much larger world, both past and present, and requires the participation of many people, both on and off the stage, to bring it to life. Without the audience and its active participation, there is no theatrical event.

Prior to the initial design conference for a production of Shakespeare's *Henry V* at the Utah Shakespearean Festival, the director, Paul Barnes, circulated several pages of introductory notes that included the following reflections on the audience:

> I don't think I know of any other play that captures so clearly the critical interdependence of playwright, actor, and audience and their collective, collabora-

> tive imaginations as does *Henry V* through the exhortations of its Chorus. Those speeches are the lesson for any of us working in the theatre and an excellent reminder of what is essential to any playgoing experience. And what I like about the Chorus speeches is that they insist on *working hard*. There is no "sit-back-and-be-a-couch-potato-while-the-white-light-of-the-t.v.-lulls-you-into-unconsciousness" about it. The Chorus asks that we *lean forward*, use our imaginations, and make an ACTIVE contribution to the proceedings—which is what we need to be doing any time we sit down in a theatre seat.

The costume designer's script notes for the production, interestingly enough, which crossed paths with the director's notes in the mail, contained the following observation:

> The "wooden O" speech: Although I suspect we usually focus on what the Chorus has to say about the setting, there are lines which accurately describe the relationship between the audience at any play and the actions of every play: *Think, when we talk of horses, that you see them* and *For 'tis your thoughts that now must deck our kings*, and *Turning th' accomplishment of many years / Into an hourglass*; and *Admit me Chorus to this history*. Like the kids say: "Okay, Mom, let's pretend. . . ." Doesn't everything in this speech demand that the Chorus be dressed as a character playing a role outside the play? Connecting directly with the audience?

Explicitly or implicitly, every play asks a lot of its audience: to believe, imagine, listen, pretend, admit, think, wonder, respond (to say nothing of approve and applaud!). As we become more and more aware of what we expect from audiences, it only makes sense that we include them in all our conversations with the play, particularly those that arise in the course of text analysis.

In *Shakespeare: An Illustrated Stage History*, Jonathan Bate and Russell Jackson suggest that we are asking more than ever of our audiences.

> The audience in the 1990s will have seen warriors who are suspect, fairies with unresolved sexual problems, and clowns who might have been conceived by Dostoevsky and trained by Beckett. They will probably expect to be

shown the play's relevance to their own preoccupations, and its claims to be taken seriously may depend on their going home with a sceptical view of human happiness (if a comedy) or of the achievement of wisdom through suffering (if a tragedy). The production's physical resources may have rivalled those of an opera-house, or consisted of eight actors, two ladders, and six metal buckets. It is more probable now than fifty years ago that the company will have treated Shakespeare more as a collaborator than an authority, and that they want to help audiences find the means and arguments to change society for the better. On a good night, the audience may leave feeling that they have actively participated in something that engaged them directly, with a mind full of new arguments from old matter, and an appetite for more.

Design Conversations

8

In the theatre, we often presume that collaboration means agreement. I believe that too much agreement creates productions with no vitality, no dialectic, no truth. . . . I do not believe that collaboration means mechanically doing what the director dictates. Without resistance there is no fire. The Germans have a useful word that has no suitable English equivalent: *auseinandersetzung*. The word, literally "to set oneself apart from another," is usually translated into English as "argument," a word with generally negative connotations. . . . My best work emanates from *auseinandersetzung*, which means to me that to create we must set oneself apart from each other. This does not mean, "No, I don't like your approach, or your ideas." It does not mean, "No, I won't do what you are asking me to do." It means, "Yes, I will include your suggestion, but I will come at it from another angle and add these new notions."

Anne Bogart, "Terror, Disorientation and Difficulty,"
Anne Bogart Viewpoints

Design conversations are notoriously difficult. How are two or more people going to be able to see what one member of the group is seeing in his or her imagination? Here are some reflections on the challenge, which I have excerpted from conversations I have had in recent years with theatre colleagues.

It's incredibly difficult to sit around and talk about a show in visual terms and expect any two (or more) people to understand what you mean. Our vocabulary has too large a gray area. You absolutely must communicate visually with your comrades in the process. You can rarely find just the image you want, so you have to be able to pick up a pencil and sketch it out on a napkin or whatever is handy.

You can't describe a color with words alone. A choreographer once told me he wanted a shaft of red sunlight for the beginning of a ballet. I went home with a picture of a fire engine in my head, but I couldn't sleep. The fire engine seemed wrong for the piece. The next day I asked him, "What kind of red?" He couldn't find words so he just rubbed his thumb against his fingers to suggest texture and made a sound with his mouth like it was full of dust. I immediately knew exactly which color he meant. So, don't be afraid to resort to grunts and gestures; they can be very informative. At tech, when he saw the cue, he said, "That's exactly the color I was thinking of! How did you know?"

I take anything into the meetings that will help communicate most clearly with the director and other designers. It may be preliminary sketches, copies of research, images torn from this or that, swatches, whatever. No holds barred when it comes to this. Every director is different and every production is different.

I try my best to keep my eyes and ears open at all times. The more references you have at your disposal, the better off you are. Just making a routine trip to the library won't do it for me. I force myself to search for thought-provoking imagery constantly.

The presentation changes as often as the information itself. One director I've worked with responds positively to spreading out as much info as possible on the table so we can play with them, move them about, point out the most appropriate. Other times I have kept my visual ideas in a folder and presented them one at a time, to fully discuss a single photo or sketch. Sometimes one particularly striking image may have a profound effect on the final designs.

Communication, communication. I can't say that word enough. The most positive and successful relationships I have had are with directors who truly communicate with designers. Not only talking about their own thoughts and ideas but respecting and listening to the ideas of the designers. Hopefully, everyone involved in the production development has an intelligent grasp of the script, and brings their own mind and experiences to the table. I believe it is collaboration that makes our efforts as theatre artists worthwhile.

The six brief sections that follow are all examples of the different forms design conversations can take. Each example includes a visual component that relates to work in progress.

Clocks?

Kurt Daw, chair of the Department of Theatre at Kennesaw State University, reflects on a design conversation he had with scene designer, Keith Belli.

> The sketch in Figure 8–1 is by scene designer Keith Belli and was created for our Classic TheaterWorks production of *The Illusion*, by Tony Kushner. The show concerns the nature of theater itself and features a number of flashbacks,

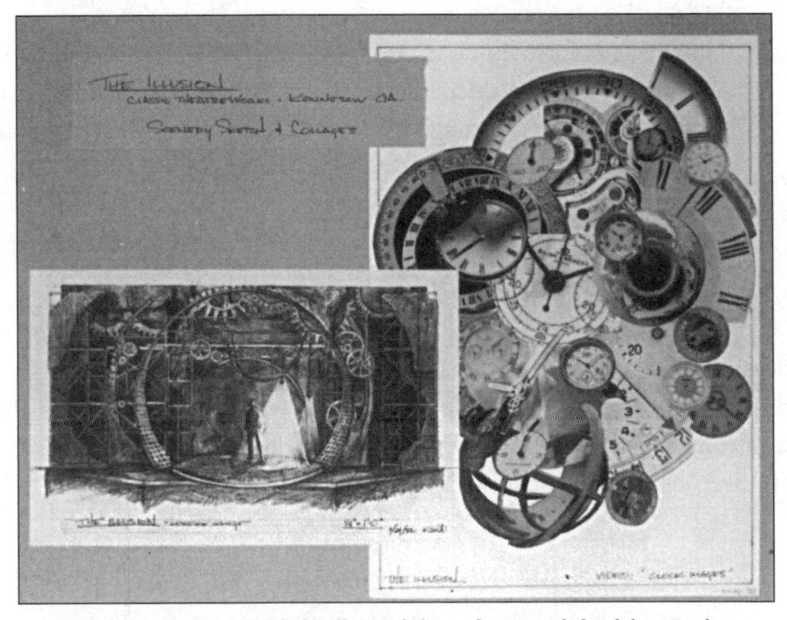

Figure 8–1. *A preparatory clock collage and the resulting pencil sketch by scene designer Keith Belli for a production of Tony Kushner's adaptation of Corneille's* The Illusion. *Photograph by Richard Ingham.*

although the man who is watching them doesn't realize he is seeing scenes from plays, mistaking them for events in the life of his estranged son in the real world.

When I first spoke to Keith about this play, I emphasized its theatrical nature. I was very interested in the stage within a stage. I was perplexed, therefore, when the first research Keith presented me with was all pictures of watches and clockwork. I confessed to Keith that I didn't know where he was going, but the images were so compelling that I told him to explore a bit more.

The next thing I got from him was this remarkable sketch. The final set looked almost exactly like this. I realized that Keith had seen that the play was really about time, its passage, and its effects on people. In my production, the play appeared to be set inside the machinery of a giant clock. The circular forms in both the vertical and horizontal planes became terrific playing spaces. Because the spaces had such great shapes, it was easy to get the theatrical story told. We made the stages-within-the-stage out of these carefully defined circles. What I would never have gotten without Keith's collaboration was the sense of time, and its passing.

This sketch was the design that taught me to be careful about dictating too directly what I want in a design. It is better to speak to designers of ideas and feelings. They sometimes bring astonishing, and unexpected, things to the table if you let their imaginations have free play.

Bulletin Boards

Remember the designer who suggested that his bulletin board was a reflection of his imagination? Figures 8–2, 8–3, and 8–4 represent several pieces of design work, which I think prove beyond a doubt that all that concentration on manipulating the elements of design with shapes, corkboard, and pushpins definitely pays off!

Figure 8–2. *Preparatory scene design collage by Keith Belli for* David's Red Haired Death *at Woolly Mammoth Theatre, Washington, D.C. Photograph by Richard Ingham.*

Figure 8–3. *Paint elevation by Keith Belli for Nicky Silver's* Fat Men in Skirts *at Woolly Mammoth Theatre, Washington, D.C. Photograph by Richard Ingham.*

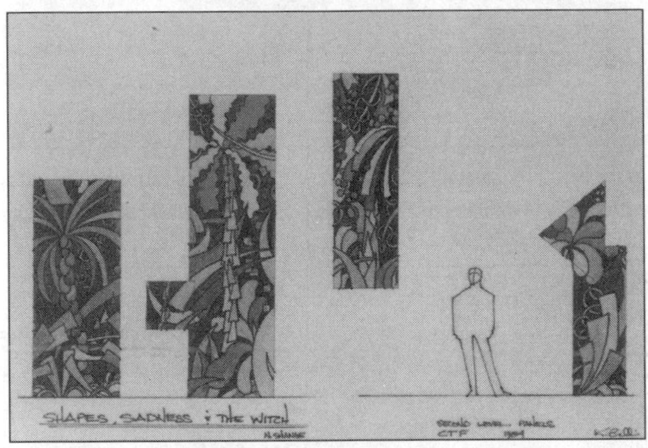

Figure 8–4. *Designs for series of panels by Keith Belli for a production of N. Shange's* Shapes, Sadness and the Witch *at the Kennedy Center Children's Theatre. Photograph by Richard Ingham.*

Cathy in Cloud Nine

When I designed the costume for Cathy in a production of *Cloud Nine* at Mary Washington College, my first step was the collage in Figure 8–5. At the beginning of act 2 of Caryl Churchill's play, a stage direction describes Cathy

Figure 8–5. *Cathy costume collage by Rosemary Ingham. Photograph by Richard Ingham.*

Figure 8–6. Cathy in Caryl Churchill's Cloud Nine, at *Actors Theatre of Louisville* with Frederic Major. Photograph by David S. Talbott.

as "Lin's daughter, age four, played by a man, clinging to Lin." They are in a park and it is chilly; Lin reminds Cathy to put on her hat. In the course of the scene, Cathy recites:

> Batman and Robin
> Had a batmobile
> Robin done a fart
> And paralyzed the wheel
> The wheel couldn't take it
> The engine fell apart
> All because of Robin
> And his supersonic fart.

These words characterized Cathy for me, informing both the collage and the final costume. Curiously enough, the hat on the actor playing Cathy in another production of *Cloud Nine* at Actor's Theatre of Louisville is very similar to the image in my collage. The character explains 'her' gender plight: "They hit me. I can't play. They said I'm a girl."

Arcadia

Paul Tazewell talks a great deal about making connections between actors and characters. He is keenly aware that, although costumes connect actors to characters, it is the actor's body that ultimately determines the final line of the costume and how it will be worn. "I can do only so much work in my imagination before I want to know exactly who's going to play the parts. I like to talk to the actors as soon as possible. I can go in knowing a lot about the play, and a lot about the period, but it's when actors begin to talk about their characters that it all begins to fall into place." The sketches in Figures 8–7, 8–8, and 8–9 are examples of the way the designer combined character information from the text and suggestions from the actors who actually played the roles in the Arena Stage production.

Figure 8–7. *Costume sketch for Tomasina by Paul Tazewell for the Arena Stage production of Tom Stoppard's* Arcadia.

Figure 8–8. *Costume sketch for Septimus by Paul Tazewell for the Arena Stage production of Tom Stoppard's* Arcadia.

TOMASINA: If you could stop every atom in its position and direction, and if your mind could comprehend all the actions thus suspended, then if you were really, *really* good at algebra you could write the formula for all the future; and although nobody can be so clever as to do it, the formula must exist just as if one could.

*

SEPTIMUS: I assure you. Mrs. Chater is charming and spirited, with a pleasing voice and a dainty step, she is the epitome of all the qualities

Figure 8–9. *Costume sketch for Noakes by Paul Tazewell for the Arena Stage production of Tom Stoppard's* Arcadia.

society applauds in her sex—and yet her chief renown is for a readiness that keeps her in a state of tropical humidity as would grow orchids in her drawers in January.

*

SEPTIMUS: Well, so much for Mr. Noakes. He puts himself forward as a gentleman, a philosopher of the picturesque, a visionary who can move mountains and cause lakes, but in the scheme of the garden he is as the serpent.

Macbeth

The following is a brief excerpt from a lengthy design conversation between designer Jamie Bullins and director Kurt Daw that informed, in part, the four sketches in Figure 8–10.

DIRECTOR: (*looking at contemporary magazine examples*) Interesting ideas. I like the gloves; I like the arms.

DESIGNER: It's sort of futuristic . . . do you want to stay away from that or . . .

DIRECTOR: I like the idea of very cutting edge. I think it's one way to get away from the specificity of any period . . . something that's maybe coming. I like the hands being covered; I always think that's sort of evocative of people who've got something to hide. Let me tell you what I think Lady Macbeth's story is: I think the central question always behind Lady Macbeth is, is she strong or is she weak? I favor the weak . . . that is, she's falling apart from the strain, almost from the beginning. She doesn't successfully evoke the spirits. She's somebody who wants a lot more than she can possibly get. She can see that Macbeth can't get it himself, so she goes after trying to help him get it but the psychic cost is too high. I think she starts falling apart fairly early. . . .

DESIGNER: I think that as Macbeth starts to fall apart it's visually evident, and I think with her it should be the opposite . . . she puts on more or she tries to keep herself together visually when inside she's deteriorating, and Macbeth doesn't care one way or the other. As he breaks down, we could definitely remove things, open things up.

DIRECTOR: This is a play about deterioration. It will be interesting to show the way that some characters fall increasingly away from clean and sharpness. They are, in general, extremely delineated people and very clear about who they are. They're also very clear about the kind of impression they're trying to make. I think this is an

Figure 8–10. *Four sketches by Jamie Bullins for a production of* Macbeth. *(a) and (b) are Macbeth; (c) is Lady Macbeth; and (d) is the Witches.*

extremely political play, and I'm interested in the politics. I'm really interested in the idea of people who attend to appearances very, very carefully.

DESIGNER: Since the set is so neutral in color, I imagine strong color on the people.

DIRECTOR: Yes. Selectively. I'm into super-saturate color statements . . . the kind of thing that makes the audience go "My God!" Even Lady Macbeth, Lady Macduff, Malcolm perhaps. My guess is selective use of color that's so strong that it's . . .

DESIGNER: Jarring?

DIRECTOR: Yes. I'm quite open to very unrealistic use of color . . . unrealistic statements in color. . . .

The Magic Flute

The final example of a design conversation in action is from lighting designer Liz Stillwell, who describes her unique contribution to a production of *The Magic Flute* at the University of California/Irvine.

> The director, Robert Cohen, the scenic designer, Douglass Scott Goheen, and the technical director, Keith Bangs, had been trying for weeks to design scenery and technical tricks to portray the Trial of Fire and Water that Tamino and Pamina must pass through at the climax of the opera. Everything they tried seemed too clunky and "solid" to be magical. They asked me if I could do "something with light" on a bare stage. (Sure!)
>
> For Fire, I designed traps with firelight and smoke flowing up, and moving flame projections on the cyclorama in amber. The projections intersected their bodies as they walked through it and projected their shadows in the flame. For Water, I specified overhead pipes to drop dry ice fog in two curtains. The flame projectors were then switched to flow downward and the color removed to create white water falling.
>
> These elements: smoke rising versus fog falling, and the same projection moving in opposite directions, worked together like two sides of the same coin. That kind of unity in design choices when creating special

(a)

(b)

Figure 8–11. *Two sketches by lighting designer Liz Stillwell for the Trial of Fire at the climax of The* Magic Flute.

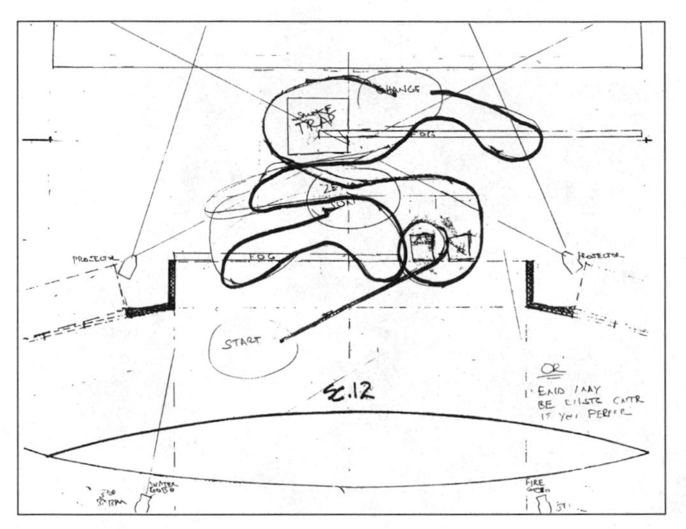

Figure 8–12. *Diagram created by Liz Stillwell to help guide the actors through her "magical environment."*

effects brings meaning to the stage picture that might otherwise be just an FX fest.

The magical environment would only work if the actors walked around the traps looking down, and through the fog curtains looking up. So, I sketched the suggested path for the director (see Figure 8–12). Later I was asked to get up on the stage and set the blocking for the actors.

Book List

The following list cites books to which I have specifically referred in each chapter, and books that have made significant contributions to my thought conversations. Like my library, this list is eclectic and highly personal.

Chapter 1

Boden, Margaret A. *The Creative Mind*. Basic Books, 1991.
Brann, Eva T. H. *The World of the Imagination*. Lanham, MD: Rowman & Littlefield, Inc., 1991.
Bruner, Jerome. *On Knowing*. Cambridge, MA: Harvard University Press, 1979.
Damasio, Antonio R. *Descartes' Error*. New York: G. P. Putnam's Sons, 1994.
Feynman, Richard P. *"What Do You Care What Other People Think?"* New York: W. W. Norton & Company, 1988.
Jackendoff, Ray. *Patterns in the Mind*. Basic Books, 1994.

Chapter 2

Austen, Jane. *Sense and Sensibility*. New York: New American Library, 1961.
Congdon, Constance. *Tales of the Lost Formicans*. New York: Broadway Play Publishing, Inc., 1989.
Delaney, Shelagh. *A Taste of Honey*. New York: Grove Press, Inc., 1959.
Dostoyevsky, Fyodor. *The Brothers Karamazov*. David Magarshack, translator. Penguin Books, 1958.
Fowles, John. *The Ebony Tower*. Boston: Little, Brown and Company, 1974.
Fugard, Athol. *Valley Song*. London: Faber and Faber, 1996.
Gems, Pam. *Stanley*. London: Nick Hern Books, 1996.
Hare, David. *Racing Demon*. London: Faber and Faber, 1990.
Hornby, Richard. *Script into Performance: A Structuralist View of Play Production*. Austin: University of Texas Press, 1977.
Ingham, Robert. *Custer*. New York: Samuel French, 1980.
Jones, Robert Edmond. *The Dramatic Imagination*. New York: Methuen Theatre Art Books, 1987.
Miller, Arthur. *Death of a Salesman*. New York: Viking Press, 1981.
O'Neill, Eugene. *Long Day's Journey into Night*. New Haven: Yale University Press, 1955.
Overmyer, Eric. *On the Verge*. New York: Broadway Play Publishing, Inc., 1986.

Potok, Chaim. *My Name Is Asher Lev.* Greenwich, CT: Fawcett Publications, Inc., 1972.
Shakespeare, William. *Hamlet* in *The Complete Works of Shakespeare.* David Bevington, ed. Glenview, IL: Scott, Foresman and Company, 1980.
Shakespeare, William. *King Lear* in *The Complete Works of Shakespeare.* David Bevington, ed. Glenview, IL: Scott, Foresman and Company, 1980.
Shakespeare, William. *Macbeth* in *The Complete Works of Shakespeare.* David Bevington, ed. Glenview, IL: Scott, Foresman and Company, 1980.
Shakespeare, William. *A Midsummer Night's Dream* in *The Complete Works of Shakespeare.* David Bevington, ed. Glenview, IL: Scott, Foresman and Company, 1980.
Silver, Nicky. *Free Will and Wanton Lust.* In manuscript.
Sophocles. *Antigone.* Translated by Lewis Galantiere from the French of Jean Anouilh. New York: Samuel French.

Chapter 3

Aristotle. *The Poetics.* W. Hamilton Fyfe and W. Rhys Roberts, translators. Cambridge, MA: Harvard University Press, 1991.
Boswell, James. *The Life of Samuel Johnson.* New Haven: Yale University Press, 1994.
Christofer, Michael. *The Shadow Box.* New York: Samuel French, 1977.
Churchill, Caryl. *Cloud Nine.* New York: Samuel French, 1979.
Grote, David. *Script Analysis: Reading and Understanding the Playscript for Production.* Belmont, CA: Wadsworth Publishing Co., 1985.
Hodge, Francis. *Play Directing: Analysis, Communication and Style.* Englewood Cliffs, NJ: Prentice-Hall, Inc., 1971.
Hornby. *Script into Performance.*
Ingham, Rosemary, and Liz Covey. *The Costume Designer's Handbook.* Portsmouth, NH: Heinemann, 1992.
Kushner, Tony. *Angels in America, Part One: Millennium Approaches.* New York: Theatre Communications Group, 1992.
Norman, Marsha. *Getting Out.* New York: Dramatists Play Service, 1979.
O'Neill. *Long Day's Journey into Night.*
Shakespeare, William. *Henry V* in *The Complete Works of Shakespeare.* David Bevington, ed. Glenview, IL: Scott, Foresman and Company, 1980.
Shakespeare, William. *Romeo and Juliet* in *The Complete Works of Shakespeare.* David Bevington, ed. Glenview, IL: Scott, Foresman and Company, 1980.
Shakespeare. *Macbeth.*
Sheridan, Richard Brinsley. *The School for Scandal.* New York: Samuel French.
Thomas, James. *Script Analysis for Actors, Directors, and Designers.* Boston: Focal Press, 1992.
Williams, Tennessee. *Cat on a Hot Tin Roof.* Baltimore: Penguin, 1976.

Chapter 4

Aristotle. *The Metaphysics*. Joe Sachs, translator. In manuscript.

Brann. *The World of the Imagination*.

Brecht, Bertolt. *Mother Courage and Her Children*. A version for the National Theatre by David Hare. London: Methuen Drama, 1995.

Demetz, Peter, ed. *Brecht: A Collection of Critical Essays*. Englewood Cliffs, NJ: Prentice Hall, Inc., 1962.

Fussell, Paul. *Wartime: Understanding and Behavior in the Second World War*. Oxford: Oxford University Press, 1989.

Gassner, John. *Form and Idea in Modern Theatre*. New York: Dryden Press, 1956.

Hays, David. *Light on the Subject: Stage Lighting for Directors and Actors—and the Rest of Us*. New York: Limelight Editions, 1989.

Hornby. *Script into Performance*.

Montaigne, Michel de. "On the Education of Children, 1579–80," in *The Complete Essays of Montaigne*. Donald M. Frame, translator. Stanford, CA: Stanford University Press, 1957.

Strayer, Joseph R., Hans W. Gatzke, and E. Harris Harbison. *The Mainstream of Civilization Since 1500*. New York: Harcourt Brace Jovanovich, Inc., 1974.

Willett, John. *The Theatre of Bertolt Brecht*. New York: New Directions, 1959.

Witt, Hubert, ed. *Brecht as They Knew Him*. New York: International Publishers, 1974.

Chapter 5

Aristotle. *The Poetics*.

Austin, Gayle. *Feminist Theories for Dramatic Criticism*. Ann Arbor: University of Michigan Press, 1990.

Birch, David. *The Language of Drama, Critical Theory and Practice*. New York: St. Martin's Press, 1991.

Clark, Barrett H. *European Theories of the Drama*. New York: Crown Publishers, 1965.

Eagleton, Terry, *Literary Theory: An Introduction*. Minneapolis: University of Minnesota Press, 1983.

Gassner. *Form and Idea in Modern Theatre*.

Hornby. *Script into Performance*.

Jones. *The Dramatic Imagination*.

Kermode, Frank. *Selected Prose of T. S. Eliot*. New York: Harcourt Brace Jovanovich, 1975.

Liberman, M. M., and Edward E. Foster. *A Modern Lexicon of Literary Terms*. Glenview, IL: Scott, Foresman and Company, 1968.
Saint-Denis, Michel. *Theatre: The Rediscovery of Style*. New York: Theatre Arts Books, 1960.
Shakespeare. *Henry V.*
Tompkins, Jane P. *Reader-Response Criticism: From Formalism to Post-Structuralism*. Baltimore: Johns Hopkins University Press, 1980.

Chapter 6

Appia, Adolphe. *The Work of Living Art and Man Is the Measure of All Things*. Coral Gables: University of Miami Press, 1960.
Bentley, Joanne. *Hallie Flanagan: A Life in the American Theatre*. New York: Alfred A. Knopf, 1988.
Brockett, Oscar G., and Robert Findlay. *Century of Innovation*. Boston: Allyn and Bacon, 1991.
Chin, Daryl. "Asian Performance Tradition and Contemporary Cultural Reality," in *Performing Arts Journal*, January 1995.
Craig, Edward Gordon. *On the Art of the Theatre*. Chicago: Browne's Bookstore, 1911.
Flanagan, Hallie. *Arena*. New York: Limelight Editions, 1985.
Whitman, Walt. *Democratic Vistas*. Kjobenhavn: Karl Schonbergs Forlag, 1874.

Chapter 7

Aristotle. *The Poetics*.
Bate, Jonathan, and Russell Jackson, editors. *Shakespeare: An Illustrated Stage History*. Oxford: Oxford University Press, 1996.
Brook, Peter. *The Empty Space*. New York: Atheneum, 1968.
Cicero. *De Republica*. Cambridge: Cambridge University Press, 1995.
Cohen, Robert. *Theatre*. Mountain View, CA: Mayfield Publishing Co., 1994.
Damashek, Barbara, and Molly Newman. *Quilters*. New York: Dramatists Play Service, 1986.
Hansen, Brian. *Theatre: The Dynamics of the Art*. Englewood Cliffs, NJ: Prentice-Hall, Inc., 1991.
Hodge. *Play Directing*.
Jones. *The Dramatic Imagination*.
Jonson, Ben. *Every Man Out of His Humour* in *The Selected Plays of Ben Jonson*. Cambridge: Cambridge University Press, 1989.

Plato. *The Republic*. Allan Bloom, translator. New York: Basic Books, 1968.
Rousseau, Jean-Jacques. *Politics and the Arts* in *Political Writings*. Madison, WI: University of Wisconsin Press, 1986.
Schlissel, Lillian. *Women's Diaries of the Westward Journey*. New York: Schocken Books, 1982.
Tocqueville, Alexis de. *Democracy in America*. New York: Alfred A. Knopf, 1945.

Chapter 8

Bogart, Anne. *Viewpoints*. Michael Bigelow Dixon and Joel A. Smith, eds. Lyme, NH: Smith and Kraus, Inc., 1995.
Stoppard, Tom. *Arcadia*. London: Faber and Faber, 1993.